Daniel R. Lee's

THE NELSON BOYS

The Nelson Boys

By Daniel R. Lee

Compiled and Edited
by
Clive Palmer

First published in Great Britain in 2019 by:
Dane Valley Press
Cheshire
UK

Compiled and edited by Clive Palmer

Front cover: *Street Scene* from
iStock.com/peeterv

Legal Deposit:
A copy of this book is held by the British Library

ISBN: 978-1-9161075-0-2

To my wife, my son's and my daughter.
Family truly is the most wonderful gift a
man can have. Every chapter I have ever
lived within my lifetime has been driven by
the love of my family, past and present.

In fond memory of my sister Lorraine and cousin Alanda,
Mum and Dad; Pam and Dickie Lee.

You can learn to live without someone,
but it doesn't stop it hurting

Contents

Images of New Addington

Drawing inspiration from social surroundings, a selection of images from the New Addington Estate are included to inform the story:

- Behind the shops on the New Estate

- The Timebridge Centre

- New Estate shops

- Applegarth

- Northwalk

- Foxcombe

- Brierley

- Coppins

- Warbank

- Elmside

All photographs by: Daniel R. Lee

Run credits

Acknowledgements

In bringing this book to publication a sincere debt of gratitude is owed to many family, friends and colleagues from my personal and professional life. Too numerous for all to be listed here, omission by name is by no means a lack of recognition for all those who have provided inspiration in conversations, however fleeting; from school-days, on film sets, in the football world and Higher Education. Thank you to you all.

To my family for their love and support in this venture and many others in my working life, often taking me far from home on too many occasions. To my wife, Julie Lee for her faith in me and spectacular patience, for always being by my side to see a project through. To my children, Daniel, William, Amy, Callum, Alfie, Freddie and Vinnie, thank you for your encouragement, for putting up with my stories and not least, tolerating my long absences at the computer whilst at home. To my sisters and brother-in-law's, Lorraine and Malachy McNally, Jackie and Andy Murray, Debbie and Les Gillam, beware, you are all in this story too, somewhere. Similarly, thanks are due to other family members, filtering in to my larger-than-life characterisations; Fred and Pat Gosling, Alan and Linda Gosling. Thanks also to close friends for fuelling my already vivid imagination with memories from the New Addington Estate in Croydon and beyond, Arron Tarry, Tom Woodcock, Darren Hoskins, and also to Steve Sallis, from www.solutionsmindset.com for his moral support and straight talking in life and in football (if there is a difference).

For their technical support, critical feedback and generosity in time spent to help me shape the episodes, and then publish this book, my heartfelt thanks are to Anita Wood, Hayley McIlroy, Al Street and Andrew Raines for proof reading the text, Ian Doughty for his artistic input, Dan Green at Trimpanda.com for the website design www.thenelsonboys.co.uk Nicholas Bolt for legal advice and Lee Cole, my business partner at Sports Education and Training Ltd., thanks for taking the helm whilst my mind and body have been elsewhere – often physically in another country or my thoughts tied up in some action between episodes five and six. Last but not least to Clive Palmer from Dane Valley Press who has shared his experience not only in editing books but promoting the interests of a keen but novice learner like me. This book has only been made possible by Clive saying 'don't just talk about it, do it!'. So, what was once a dream, has become a reality, I cannot thank you enough.

Finally, to Mum and Dad, Pam and 'Dickie' Lee who are not here to share this story but I know would be so proud. They helped me more than they could ever realise, from cherishing family values, to on-set professionalism in the film industry, they set the bar high for me, thank you for your spirit, support and love.

Run trailer

Purpose of the script

Although this script (screenplay) has been created to tell a story, it is also a working technical document, which guides the film making process. General technical terms and definitions guide the script and aid the plotline; however, there are limits for how much guidance should be offered. Occasionally scriptwriters offer more than just the dialogue by including camera shots and angles to direct the action. Generally, the more technical elements of the film making process should be left to the director, and only used within the written script when absolutely necessary. Scriptwriters should try to limit the artistic input and use the basic directions, such as locations, scene headings and dialogue. At the start of each scene, the writer will establish the setting using what is more commonly known as a 'slug line' or 'master scene header' (placed in bold in our text). This tells the reader where the scene is taking place. Slug lines will usually offer three main pieces of information, location, time of day and if the scene is indoors or outside. Slug lines are written in capital letters and also numbered in chronological order to guide the reader through the script. Firstly, the slug line will establish if the scene is an interior (INT) or exterior (EXT), then where the specific action is taking place and the time of day. Characters' names appear in upper case each time they are seen in the script indicating their entrances and exits during scene and/or screenplay. Upper case is also used to highlight important objects within the story line.

Considering the above, this script as we present it, has been dramatised to offer the reader a rich descriptive narrative and an insight to the directive elements that a working script might have during the filmmaking process. Character direction (placed in brackets, italicised text, under the character name or during their dialogue) has been introduced to make the script easier to follow in terms of the intended emotions, actions and movements to be played by the actors. Again, as a general rule for a scriptwriter, this is not common practice. Below, a glossary of film related terms is included to equip the reader with some technical screenplay jargon, and in so doing, provide some deeper appreciation of the intended emotions, movements and atmosphere which actors will be trying to portray, to tell the story of the Nelson Boys. It will also give some procedural understanding within the film making process.

Picking up the storyline...

For the first time in twenty years, Vince Nelson returns to his South London estate from his self-exile to Thailand (via prison). There are a number of reasons he has not returned before, reasons that will soon become apparent. Vince is one of seven parentless brothers, brothers who have had to fend for themselves in a corrupt, isolated environment. Vince now finds himself at his brother Danny's bedside in hospital, where he is fighting for his life. Danny is said to have been a victim of a mugging, or at least this is what the Nelson Boys are told.

In his search for answers, Vince is on a one-man mission to get to the bottom of what has happened to Danny. However, Vince is about to discover he's been deserted by his closest friends, lied to by the people he loves, cheated on by the ones he holds dearest and punished for things he hasn't done. Vince has a tough reputation and a violent background and now, with a reason for returning, things are about to get interesting…

Lights, Camera, Action
Glossary

CRANE	High shot: using a crane will give you an extremely high shot, where the camera is mounted onto a long mechanical arm.
CU	Close up: used to capture facial expressions that can be pivotal to the story plot.
DOLLY	This is a moving platform on a set of wheels that runs either on TRACK (tracking shot) or on boards, where the Grip will move to set positions in relation to the action being filmed. If the Camera Operator needs to PUSH IN on the action, the Grip will move the Dolly towards the subjects. Equally, if the requirements are to PULL BACK from the subjects or action, the Grip will move the Dolly away. If the camera needs to go higher during the shot, the Grip will JIB up (or down respectively) using a hydraulic arm that raises or lowers the camera on the vertical axis.
ESTABLISHING SHOT	Establishing where the action will take place.
F/B	Flashback: this can either be within the scene header or within the narrative, to depict action that has happened in the past.
FOCUS	Or pull focus: keeping a person or object sharp and well-defined, this can change from one actor to another during the scene with either a FOCUS SHIFT or PULL FOCUS.
FRAME	Artistic composition for the camera.
FREEZE	The effect of halting the action like a still photograph.
INTERCUT	This is used to transition between two scenes that are shown back and forth, for the purpose of keeping the scene dynamic.

MOS Mit Out Sound [mute]: Moment of Silence for dramatic effect.

O.C. Off camera: this can sometimes be O.S. (off screen), and denotes that the actor speaking is not in the shot.

OTS Over The Shoulder: can also be written as OS and is a directive for setting the frame over a character's shoulder.

PAN When the camera moves horizontally on a stationary axis.

POV Point Of View: this is where we see the action from the perspective of a character within the scene.

SHOT Is the expression of movement, ideas and emotion through camera angles and composition.

SPLIT SCREEN Is where the screen is split into two or more frames. This can be used if two people are having a telephone conversation, and can show simultaneous reactions.

TILT When the camera moves vertically on a stationary axis.

TIME SKIP This allows the scriptwriter to skip irrelevant detail within the narrative, without the story losing momentum.

UNFREEZE The effect of resuming the action after it has been frozen.

V.O. Voice Over: character narrative that can be heard over a scene.

ZOOM Changing focal length and artistic angle during the SHOT, making the object seem either nearer or further away.

Episode 1

The journey home

INTRODUCTION: OPENING MONOLOGUE

What is life? What's it all about? That is the unanswered question. I'll tell you what life is to me. It's a meaningless parody of bullshit and bravado, it's a struggle of conformity and rules, its regulations and people playing the game as they follow one another like sheep. Trying to make sense of their meaningless lives and then trying to justify it with material things that will be worth absolutely nothing in tomorrow's world. People spend their whole life doing the same mundane thing day after day serving one master like a slave. Nah, not me, I'm different, I'm lost. In fact, I've lost my faith in humanity. I've been deserted by my closest friends, lied to by the people I love, beaten to a pulp for having morals, cheated on by the ones I hold dearest and punished for things I haven't even done. That's why I feel the way I do, those are the scars only I can see. So, that's what life is to me. You on the other hand may be different. Anyway, what do I know? Besides, who am I and what right have I got to preach these pearls of wisdom to you? Well, in case you're interested, I'm Vince Nelson, and this is my story.

**Do not judge my story by the chapter you walk in on
- Unknown author**

1   **EXT. STREET O/S THE NELSON'S HOUSE – NIGHT.**   1

EPISODE 1 - The journey home

POV - The camera staggers up a DAMP, DARK and DIRTY
STREET, no different to most typical SUBURBAN
COUNCIL ESTATES in LONDON. Only the STREET LAMPS
lighting the DANK NARROW ROADS, it's WET, COLD and
eerily SILENT. Painful groaning breaks the silence,
a silhouette of a young man (DANNY) staggers up the
wet road clutching at his stomach. His breath is
visible in the damp night's air; his breathing is
irregular as he struggles to draw each breath. He
staggers aimlessly towards one of the houses on the
street. A blood soaked hand enters frame and feebly
bangs on the door. After a moment, impatiently bangs
again, this time the hand slides down the door and
out of frame leaving a bloody smear behind, he
wearily slumps against the doorframe, the door opens
and GEORGE appears in the shaft of light now coming
from the house.

                    GEORGE
                (Shocked and frantic)
        Danny, Danny, oh my god, Danny.

Danny falls into frame as George collects him in his
arms.

FADE TO BLACK.

CREDITS ROLL - TITLE MUSIC.

2   **INT. TRAIN – DAY.**   2

THE PICTURESQUE ENGLISH COUNTRYSIDE FLASHES BY
OUTSIDE THE CARRIAGE WINDOW, as the train is in full
motion heading towards London. The midday train is
busy, but VINCE sits alone at a table with a four
pack of economically priced beer for company. He is
just gazing out of the window at the bleakness of
the wind and rain. Swigging one of his beers, he has
time to reflect.

MUSIC FADES.

END OF CREDITS.

                    VINCE (V.O.)
     Well, this is a journey I thought I'd never
     take again. It's funny how things turn out.
     I've been away for a while, well almost
     twenty years, with no real intention of
     returning. This country has changed, it's
     had it, it's dirty overcrowded and the kids
     are full of attitude. I never thought I'd
     say it but I'm glad I moved abroad, what a
     shame. Mind you the system never really
     done me any favor's here. In fact, nobody
     ever really done me any favour's.

TWO YOUTHS, hoods up casually sit at the table opposite
Vince.

                    YOUTH 1
                 (With attitude)
     Alright mate, wanna give me one of those
     beers?

Vince slowly looks at them, annoyed that he has been
disturbed.

                    VINCE
          (Screwing, shocked at the audacity)
     What?

                    YOUTH 1
              (Now slightly unnerved)
     Err, the beers on the table.

The young lad points at the beers.

                    VINCE
     (Stern, slowly putting his beer on the table)
     I've got an idea lads, how's about you two
     fuck off before I knock the fuck out the
     both of ya
     (Pausing to lean forward)
     Mate.

Vince shoots them another stern look as the boys get
up and move off quickly, Vince smiles to himself
before looking back out of the window to continue
his reflections.

> VINCE (V.O.)
I got a call from my brother George saying that my little brother Danny was in hospital, and that he had taken a right pasting. Like I said before it's been a while, and believe me I've got my reasons, but it's now a case of having to go home. See I come from a big family, seven brothers including me. MUM passed away giving birth to my youngest brother FREDDIE and my DAD passed away while I was in prison.

3   **INT. HOSPITAL ROOM - DAY.**   3

High wide shot of the five brothers sitting around a hospital bed, George, FRANK, BILLY, JACK and Freddie. Danny is motionless in the bed with an oxygen mask covering his mouth and nose, IV lines in each arm replacing the fluids and blood he has lost. Leads and connectors cover his chest and arms feeding back his vital signs displayed on a large monitor above the bed.

> VINCE (V.O. CONT'D)
These are my brothers.

The camera WHIP PANS onto each brother then FREEZES on each as Vince narrates.

> VINCE (V.O.)
That's Danny in the bed, Danny's in his mid-twenties. He's a bit of a wide boy. He came to see me in Thailand last year and pretty much pissed it up from the moment he arrived, but he's a good kid. That's George holding Danny's hand. George is the eldest at forty-five, two years older than me. I think George had it the hardest when Dad died. I was inside and with Mum gone, George brought the other boys up all on his own. I respect him, I really respect him, we all do. That's Frank texting on his phone at the back of the room, Frank is a year younger than me and lives about ten miles away from our family home. He's done alright for himself, he owns a small business. He was always gonna do alright

the tight fucker. That's Billy sitting the
other side of Danny with his head in his
hands. Billy is thirty-five, he lives in
Portsmouth these days, gave the Navy a go
but got slung out. Losing Mum and Dad
really hit him hard. He drinks himself
silly to numb the pain, shame really he's a
decent bloke and a lot shrewder than people
give him credit for. That's Jack with his
feet on the end of the bed falling asleep.
Jack's in his early thirties and still at
home. Without Jack's money coming in George
would proper struggle, Jack works hard and
plays hard, oh yeah and he's bit of a
ladies' man, or at least he thinks he is.
That's little Freddie leaning on George,
Freddie is only just in his twenties and
still at home with Danny, George and Jack.
Not much I can tell you about the lad, he
was five when I went away and the only
times I've seen him was when George brought
him out to Thailand when he was a little
kid. Other than that a few brief
conversations on the phone and the odd
text, that's it.

                    TICKET INSPECTOR (V.O.)
          Ticket please.

4   INT. TRAIN CONT. – DAY.   4

The ticket inspector stands over Vince who is still
deep in thought. Vince snaps out of his solitude and
looks at the inspector, who smiles at him.

                    TICKET INSPECTOR
                         (Smiling)
          Ticket please.

Vince smiles back, leans to one side and pulls a
ticket out from his back pocket.

                    TICKET INSPECTOR
               (Taking, then clipping the ticket)
          In a world of your own their son.

OTS - Vince looks up.

                         VINCE
                 (Tiredly rubs his eyes)
        Yeah, seems that way.

The ticket inspector stamps the ticket and hands
it back.

                    TICKET INSPECTOR
                       (Smiling)
        Thank you young man, have a great day.

The inspector moves off.

                         VINCE
                  (Almost to himself)
        Cheers mate.

Vince sits back and empties his beer, reaches for
another and starts to reflect again.

5   **INT. HOSPITAL ROOM CONT'D. – EVENING.**   5

It's now into the late evening and the Nelson boys
are still around the bed, starting to get a little
agitated.

                         FRANK
                        (Tired)
        Did you actually speak to Vince?

                         GEORGE
                       (Yawning)
        I've left him a couple of messages; he may
        well have tried to ring the house, but
        he'll be well on his way by now.

                        FREDDIE
                  (Curious, to Jack)
        Do you think he'll come?

                         GEORGE
                (Assertive and assuring)
        He'll be here.

George puts an arm around Freddie to comfort him. A
NURSE knock's and enters. Jack stands sharply. She
looks around the room then exchanges a smile with
Jack before heading towards George.

                    NURSE
                  (Softly)
The tests are in and everything seems to be
fine at the moment. He will however remain
unconscious for a few days, this is because
of the medication, but the Doctor will
speak to you in the morning and update you
on his progress. Please Mr Nelson, go home
and rest.

                   GEORGE
             (Turning to the boys)
Ok you heard, go home, I'll stay with Dan.

                    NURSE
                  (Concerned)
You really need to rest too Mr. Nelson.

She puts a reassuring hand on his shoulder.

                    FRANK
(Placing his hand on George's other shoulder)
You heard her, he's going to be ok for
tonight, he's being well looked after. Come
on, there's nothing we can do sitting here.
Let's have a pint and get some rest.

Billy suddenly looks up once Frank mentions beer.

                    NURSE
                (Reassuringly)
He's right Mr. Nelson, there's not much you
can do, we will call you if things change.

George nods reluctantly and agrees. The nurse exits.
George stands over Danny and holds his hand.

                   GEORGE
     (Caringly, kissing Danny on the forehead)
I won't be far mate, I promise.

The boys exit, HIGH WIDE SHOT high wide shot of
Danny alone surrounded by the MEDICAL EQUIPMENT. He
is in the solitude of total silence.

6 INT. HOSPITAL CORRIDOR – NIGHT.   6

As the boys head for the front of the hospital, two
well-dressed men walk past them in the corridor.
DETECTIVE INSPECTOR PATTERSON and DETECTIVE SERGEANT
DELGADO.

>   DI PATTERSON
>   *(Calling after them)*
>   Mr. Nelson.

All the brothers stop in unison, they then look back
as the men slowly approach them.

Camera swiftly pushes in on a CU of Patterson then
FREEZES while Vince narrates.

>   VINCE (V.O.)
>   Now, as far as people go, this man is the
>   biggest scumbag god ever put breath in to.
>   I've got my reasons to dislike him, ones
>   that will soon become apparent. But this
>   man, you just cannot trust on any level.

UNFREEZE. Patterson offers his hand out for George
to shake.

>   DI PATTERSON
>   *(Smugly)*
>   George if I remember rightly?

George shakes his hand reluctantly.

>   GEORGE
>   *(Confused)*
>   That's right, and you are?

>   DI PATTERSON
>   *(Smiling smugly)*
>   I'm DI Patterson and this is DS Delgado

Delgado shakes George's hand and smiles politely.

>   DI PATTERSON (CONT'D)
>   I was wondering if we could have a few
>   words

DI Patterson looks around at the brothers.

                    DI PATTERSON (CONT'D)
                    (Smiling insincerely)
          In private.

George looks around at his brothers who have now
stood tall in unity, almost like peacocks showing
their feathers.

                         GEORGE
                         (Firm)
          I've told the officers that were here
          yesterday everything I know.

George smiles back insincerely, and then turns to
walk away.

Patterson Grabs George's arm, stopping him and turns
him back around.

                       DI PATTERSON
          Maybe you should tell me what you know?

The brothers all move in closer, standing strong
together.

                         GEORGE
              (Pulling his arm from Patterson's grip)
          Are you asking me or telling me?

                       DI PATTERSON
                    (With a forced smile)
          When you're ready of course Mr. Nelson. I
          know now is not a good time.

                         GEORGE
                 (Walking away with his brothers)
          Maybe another time.

The Nelson boys walk out of the hospital doors as
Patterson and Delgado watch on inquisitively.

                       DI PATTERSON
                       (To himself)
          Yeah, you can bet your life on it George.

Delgado then looks at Patterson curiously, as
Patterson watches the Nelson's leave.

7   INT/EXT. THE MOON PUB - EVENING.   7

The Nelson boys enter the pub. It is a typically
quiet Monday night.

                    JACK
        You boys sit down, I'll get us a pint. Come
        on Freddie give me a hand.

Jack and Freddie head to the bar, the others move
over toward a table and sit. While this is going on
there are a few lads around the other side of the
bar making a lot of noise.

Jack and Freddie approach the bar, LENNY is tending.

                    JACK
            (Pulling money from his pocket)
        Alright Lenny?

                    LENNY
            (Turning to face them)
        Alright Jack, what can I get ya?

Jack Looks over to the table calculating what he
needs.

                    JACK
        The usual for me mate, Freddie and George
        will have a Guinness, err, a lager top and
        a coke please Len.

                    LENNY
            (Pouring the drinks)
        Sorry to Hear about Danny, how's he doing?

                    JACK
        He seems to be ok for now, just waiting to
        find out who did it.

                    LENNY
            (Sincerely)
        I'll keep my ear to the ground Jack, if I
        hear anything I'll let you know.

                    JACK
      (Pointing at the beers Lenny has poured)
Take them over Fred. (To Lenny) Yeah cheers
Len, It's appreciated.

                    LENNY
              (At the till)
That's eighteen forty please Jack.

                    JACK
      (Sarcastic, handing the money over)
Fuck me Len! Even Dick Turpin wore a mask.

They exchange a smile. Jack gives Lenny the cash
then heads over to join his brothers at the table.

                   GEORGE
              (Confused)
It's still bugging me, I know that cozzer
from somewhere.

                    JACK
              (Agreeing)
Yeah, he did look familiar.

The lads at the other end of the bar SMASH A GLASS,
they then fall about LAUGHING, and the brothers look
over.

                   FRANK
           (Looking at the lads)
Who's that lot?

                    JACK
That's SAMMY KEPPEL and his mob.

                   BILLY
Keppel, as in RONNIE KEPPEL?

                  FREDDIE
            (Taken back a bit)
Yeah, Ronnie is Sammy's Dad. How do you
know Ronnie Keppel?

                   BILLY
Your brother Vince used to knock about with
him.

                    FREDDIE
               (Impressed)
     I didn't know Vince hung around with the
     top boys.

                    BILLY
          (Looking at Frank and laughing)
     Fucking top boys, Ronnie, do me a favour!

                    GEORGE
               (Butting in)
     Well things changed Bill. Ronnie got
     tangled up with CHARLIE MADIGAN when Vince
     went away.

                    BILLY
               (Falling in)
     Oh so Sammy is Ronnie Keppel and LUCY
     MADIGAN'S kid?

                    GEORGE
     Yeah, that's right.

                    BILLY
               (Smirking)
     Things are going to be interesting when
     Vince gets here, very fucking interesting.

                    FRANK
               (Disgusted)
     I reckon that old shitter is the reason he
     never came home. Slag never even waited for
     the verdict.

                    FREDDIE
               (Confused)
     For Vince's verdict? Wait, I don't
     understand.

Freddie looks around his brothers for an answer.

                    FREDDIE (CONT'D)
               (Intrigued)
     What's Vince got to do with all this lot?

                    GEORGE
               (Shooting Frank a look)
     Nice one Frank.

George Turns to Freddie and settles, ready to tell
him the story.

                    GEORGE
     Well, Vince and Sammy's Mum used to be,
     well, let's just say that they used to be
     good friends.

                    FREDDIE
                (Shaking his head)
     I'm in my fucking twenties George, I do
     know what you mean.

The lads smile and share the moment.

                    GEORGE
                (Starting again)
     Anyway, they went out together for a few
     years but Lucy's old man…

                    FREDDIE
             (Eagerly, interrupting)
     Charlie Madigan!

                    GEORGE
             (Regaining momentum)
     Yeah, Charlie Madigan. Well, Charlie
     stopped Lucy from having anything to do
     with Vince, and believe me he certainly
     made sure she never got near him. Anyway,
     after Vince was sentenced Lucy and Ronnie
     got together. After a few months, she was
     pregnant with Sammy, then they got married,
     and now they live happily ever after.

                    FRANK
                (Chipping in)
     The only reason Charlie had Ronnie around
     was because at the time he was a wannabe
     gangster.

                    GEORGE
          (Abrupt looking back at Frank)
     Yeah thanks Frank, shall I finish the story
     or not.

                    FRANK
              (*Smirking*)
Sorry, continue.

                    GEORGE
         (*Getting into the story again*)
Anyway, six or so months after that Dad had
his heart attack and died, 'course Vince
was banged up with all this going on.

                    FREDDIE
            (*Trying to keep up*)
Vince must have been screwing. He must have
gone mad.

                    GEORGE
              (*Continuing*)
Yeah, and to top it off Vince was denied
the right to attend Dad's funeral. I reckon
that is one of the biggest reason he has
never been back, there's far too many bad
memories for him here.

                    BILLY
            (*Swigging his pint*)
Well he's coming back now, and I know a few
people that won't be best pleased to see
him.

                    JACK
I hope he does come.

                    GEORGE
            (*Reassuringly firm*)
He'll be here, but I warn you all now, no
trouble.

                    FREDDIE
              (*Curious*)
Will he start trouble then do you reckon?

                    BILLY
       (*Looking at Freddie amused knowingly*)
Who, your brother?

                    FREDDIE
              (*Eagerly*)
Yeah.

                    BILLY
Trouble seems to find him wherever he goes,
besides, your brother don't start trouble,
he finishes it.

The conversation is interrupted. Sammy and his
cronies abuse Lenny the barman.

                    SAMMY
              (Cocky and loud)
Len give us another round, oh and pick this
glass up while you're at it.

                    LENNY
            (Slightly embarrassed)
Alright Sammy, I'll pour your drinks first,
ok?

                    SAMMY
                  (Rude)
No you fucking moron, clear the glass up
first (turning to his friends and gesturing
toward Lenny with his thumb), wanker.

The brothers look on from across the bar.

                    BILLY
                 (Annoyed)
That's one mouthy little prick.

Billy looks over at Lenny getting a dustpan.

               BILLY (CONT'D)
                 (Curious)
Is that Lenny Hodge?

                    JACK
Yeah.

                    BILLY
                (Surprised)
What the fuck happened to him? Look how old
he looks.

                    GEORGE
      (To Freddie, gesturing toward Lenny)
See your brother Vince and Ronnie used to
knock around with Lenny.

                    FRANK
                 (Chipping in)
    Well your brother took Lenny under his wing
    and made sure nobody took liberties with
    him, they actually got on really well.

                    BILLY
                 (To Freddie)
    You must know him Fred?

Billy points toward Sammy.

                    FREDDIE
    Yeah and you were right Bill, he is a
    prick. But with that big mush always there,
    nobody takes the piss with him.

The boys all look over at who is with Sammy.

                    FRANK
    Who is the big fella, he's a fucking unit?

THE CAMERA WHIP PANS ONTO MARCUS, THEN FREEZES.

                    JACK (V.O.)
    His name is MARCUS. He works for Ronnie and
    his only job is to makes sure Sammy don't
    get himself into any trouble.

UNFREEZE.

                    GEORGE
    They reckon he can have a tear up.

As Lenny bends over to pick up the glass, one of the
boys pushes him over with their foot while he
crouches. They all laugh. Billy stands up from the
table.

                    BILLY
              (Annoyed, to his brothers)
    Fuck this, that's enough.

Billy quickly heads over to where Sammy and co are,
Jack and Frank follow reluctantly.

                    BILLY (CONT'D)
                 (*To Sammy and co*)
     That's enough of that lads, you've had your
     fun.

Billy and Jack get Lenny to his feet.

                      SAMMY
      (*Shoulders back, fronting the Nelson boys*)
     Says who?

Marcus and co come forward as do the brothers.

                      BILLY
                 (*Fronting up*)
     Says me.

Jack puts his arm across Billy's chest, holding him
back.

                      JACK
               (*Calming the situation*)
     Look, we ain't here for any trouble Sammy,
     he's just looking out for Lenny, that's
     all.

Freddie pushes his way to the front and steps
between Sammy and Billy.

                     FREDDIE
                  (*Explaining*)
     Hold up boys, like Jack said, we aren't
     here for any trouble, we've had a long day
     that's all.

The tension eases slightly.

                     FREDDIE
                  (*Explaining*)
     My brother was just making sure Lenny was
     ok, he never meant anything by it.

                      JACK
                (*Trying to defuse*)
     Yeah, sorry about that Sammy. Look, we've
     got a lot going on right now, we can't be
     doing with any trouble, let's just leave it
     there alright?

The boys back off slowly knowing they are well out
numbered, they head towards the bar watched by Sammy
and co.

                    LENNY
          (Recognising Billy, shaking his hand)
     Good to see ya again Bill.

                    BILLY
          (Nodding and dusting Lenny down)
     You too Len, almost didn't recognise ya.

                    LENNY
          (Whispering, looking over at Sammy)
     Yeah working for his Dad will do that to
     ya, put years on me. Try to keep out of
     their way mate, just a friendly warning.

                    BILLY
          (Not impressed and not lowering his voice)
     Fuck him and fuck his dad.

                    LENNY
              (Slightly laughing)
     You haven't changed a bit Bill, so where
     you been hiding then?

                    BILLY
     I stayed in Portsmouth when I dropped out
     of the navy mate, sort of built a life down
     there.

                    LENNY
     It's got to have been over ten years Bill.

They exchange a reminiscent smile.

                    BILLY
          (Shaking his head in almost disbelief)
     Flies by don't it.

                    GEORGE
              (Taking control)
     Right lads let's get out of here, it's been
     a long day and us ending up in the nick
     ain't gonna help Danny.

                    LENNY
                 (Sincere)
Send Danny my best and tell him I'm
thinking of him.

                   GEORGE
           (Turning to face Lenny)
Thanks mate, see ya soon.

As the boys start to leave, Sammy walks over.

                   SAMMY
                (Insincere)
Yeah, I hope Danny feels better soon
Freddie.

The boys turn to face Sammy, who has now been joined
by Marcus.

                  FREDDIE
                 (Uneasy)
Err, yeah thanks.

                   SAMMY
                 (Cocky)
Send him my regards won't ya.

Jack ensures Billy and Frank walk out then turns
back.

                    JACK
               (Fronting up)
I will Sam (they look eye to eye for a
moment, without breaking eye contact Jack
calls over to Lenny) goodnight Len.

                   LENNY
                 (Waving)
Goodnight Jack.

Jack breaks eye contact and leaves, Sammy and Marcus
watch them go.

8   EXT. GRAVEYARD – EXT.   8

HIGH WIDE CRANE SHOT – (Vince narrating throughout)
the graveyard is eerie and soundless. Vince is
silhouetted against the perimeter wall as he walks
toward one particular gravestone. OTS we reveal a
gravestone illuminated in the moonlight as he
arrives. Vince takes a deep breath, stoops to clear
a few dead leaves to reveals his parents' names.

                    VINCE (V.O.)
        I often tended my Mother's grave, mostly
        with my Dad. That seems a lifetime ago now.
        My Father and I were close, we had a
        special bond, I worshiped the ground he
        walked on, and I really did. I couldn't
        begin to tell you what I went through the
        day I found out he had died. Closure,
        that's what George says I need. I think
        that's all bollocks, what's done is done
        and saying goodbye is like leaving someone
        behind. I ain't ready to leave anyone
        behind.

Emotionally Vince wipes a small tear from his eye,
kisses his hand and places it on the headstone.

9   EXT. STREETS – NIGHT.   9

The Nelson boys walk along the DIMLY LIT PATH,
nearing a PARADE OF SHOPS on their way home.

                    FREDDIE
            (Putting his arm around George)
        I am proper starving, you gonna knock
        something up when we get home?

                    GEORGE
            (Shrugging his arm off)
        I ain't cooking this time of night Fred, if
        you want to eat, stop at the kebab shop.

                    FREDDIE
            (Mock pleading)
        Oh please George, you know I'm proper
        skint.

                    FRANK
              (Chipping in blunt)
        Why don't you make your own grub? You ain't
        a baby Fred.

Freddie glances over at Jack and smirks as Jack
gestures 'wanker' behind Frank's back. Frank turns
to speak to George.

                    FRANK (CONT'D)
        You do far too much for these boys George,
        you should tell them to piss off every now
        and then.

                    GEORGE
              (Defending the boys)
        I don't mind Frank, anyway if I don't look
        after them who will?

                    FRANK
              (Shaking his head)
        They are big enough and ugly enough to look
        after themselves. (Calling to the others
        who have walked on a bit) Boys stop at
        Arek's, and Jack will buy you all a kebab.

Frank turns to Jack.

                    FRANK (CONT'D)
                  (Smug)
        What Jack? Did you think I was gonna let
        you get away with calling me a wanker?

Frank winks at Jack, as Jack wryly smiles, knowingly
defeated. The boys sarcastically show their
appreciation, thanking Jack.

10   **EXT. GRAVEYARD/STREETS – NIGHT.**   10

LOW STATIC WIDE SHOT - VINCE DROPS INTO FRAME onto
the WET PAVEMENT from the graveyard wall with his
back to camera, FULL FRAME. He pauses to lift his
collar shielding himself from the cold night's air
and walks away from camera into the distance.

                    VINCE (V.O.)
        Well here goes, time to see the family.

11   **INT. THE MOON PUB – NIGHT.**   11

An extremely well dressed middle-aged man walks
through the pub door with a confident swagger.

                    RONNIE
              (Heading toward the bar)
     Alright Lenny?

A rhetorical question. Ronnie doesn't wait for a
response and certainly isn't interested in Lenny's
well-being.

                    LENNY
              (Looking up smiling)
     Hello boss.

Ronnie Looking around the empty bar, he then see's
Sammy and co. playing pool.

                    RONNIE
     How's it been tonight?

Ronnie has not looked at Lenny once. He opens the
till and takes out the money, flicks through it and
puts it in his suit pocket.

                    LENNY
     Quiet really, the Nelson boys popped in for
     one, other than that just Sammy and his
     mate's.

Ronnie Turns the TV off after blowing the dust from
the remote

                    RONNIE
     This place need's a fucking good scrub.

Ronnie wipes his finger across the optic's shelf and
inspects it.

                    LENNY
     I'll do that first thing Guv.

                    RONNIE
              (Looking at the broken glass in the dust pan)
     What happened?

                    LENNY
          (*Looking over at Sammy's lot and covering*)
       Oh err, nothing really.

Ronnie walk's around the bar slowly to where Sammy
and co. are, he stands there for a beat, one of
Sammy's friends nudges him and nods towards Ronnie.
He stares silently for an awkward moment as the boys
look back in anticipation.

Ronnie gently breaking the silence, with an
insincere smile.

                    RONNIE
       Boy's, I've told you before, don't fuck
       about in the pub, (leaning slowly forward,
       now nose to nose with Sammy, and further
       softening his tone) do I make myself clear
       son.

                    SAMMY
             (*Looking sheepish*)
       Crystal Dad, sorry.

                    RONNIE
          (*Smiling arrogantly and standing upright*)
       Good. Now I don't mind you lot coming in,
       but I do mind you taking the piss. I don't
       really think I need to say anymore chaps
       (looking around, as there is another
       awkward silence) well go on then vamoose.
       Go on then, fuck off.

Sammy's friends scurry around collecting their
belongings and leave quickly, Sammy and Marcus stay
seated.

                    RONNIE (CONT'D)
       Marcus, do me a favor and take him home.
       You can bring the Merc back in the morning.
       Marcus pick's his coat up and they leave.

                    RONNIE (CONT'D)
             (*Calling over to Lenny*)
       Lock up Len, I'll see you in the morning.

                    LENNY
       Will do Ronnie, goodnight.

Ronnie doesn't wait for a response and leaves as
Lenny starts to close up.

12 EXT. CAR/THE MOON PUB CARPARK – NIGHT.   12

Delgado watches Ronnie leave from his car, then gets
out and heads toward the pub.

                    DELGADO
          (Dialing a number on his mobile phone)
          (Pause) It's me (Pause) I'm on it.

He closes the phone and bangs on the door of the
pub. He looks around to check that he has not been
spotted.

13   INT/EXT. KEBAB SHOP – NIGHT.   13

Freddie and Jack playfully tussle over who will be
served first. George, Billy and Frank talk at the
back of the shop.

                    BILLY
          So what's the plan then?

                    GEORGE
             (Sticking to his guns)
          We wait.

                    BILLY
             (Slightly vexed)
          For what? Danny's in hospital and we need
          to find out who put him there, pronto.

                    FRANK
              (Cutting in)
          And fucking sort it out sharpish.

                    GEORGE
               (Firm)
          We wait for Vince and that is that.

                    FRANK
          Vince could be days away.

                    BILLY
          If he comes at all.

                          GEORGE
          Trust me, he'll be here.

14   EXT. STREET/KEBAB SHOP – NIGHT.   14

HIGH WIDE SHOT - Vince walks along the street,
silhouetted by the streetlights.

                          VINCE (V.O.)
          What the hell am I doing here? I've got a
          really bad feeling about all this. All I
          can think about is little Danny, someone is
          gonna pay?

Vince walks past a brightly illuminated doorway,
it's the previously established kebab shop, the
brothers are inside ordering their food.

15   EXT. KEBAB SHOP CONT'D – NIGHT.   15

As the three brothers continue their conversation,
unseen by them VINCE WALKS PAST IN THE BACKGROUND.

                          FRANK
          Well I hope he ain't far, 'cause this has
          really got to get sorted.

                          GEORGE
          Look, I'll call him again tomorrow.

                          AREK
                 (Calling over to George)
          Do you want salad George?

                          GEORGE
                 (Walking forward with Frank)
          No thanks mate.

                          JACK
                 (Pulling money from his wallet)
          How much is that lot mate?

Arek totals up their order as Jack prepares to pay.

16   EXT. NELSON'S HOUSE – NIGHT.   16

Vince arrives at the family home and the house is in
darkness.

                    VINCE (V.O.)
          Great no fucker home, what a warm welcome
          back after all this time.

He puts his duffle bag on the doorstep then reaches
over to open the back gate. He looks up at the
bathroom window that is slightly open.

                    VINCE (V.O.)
          Well this'll bring back a few memories.

17   INT/EXT. THE KEPPEL'S DRIVEWAY – NIGHT.   17

Sammy and Marcus are sitting in the car that is now
parked with the lights off and engine running. Sammy
has the glove box open, using it to rest on as he
makes TWO LARGE LINES OF COCAINE on a COMPACT MIRROR
with a credit card. Marcus has a SMALL METAL TUBE in
his hand waiting for him to finish.

                    MARCUS
                (In mid conversation)
          So what you thinking?

                    SAMMY
            (Obviously talking about Danny)
          I think he took the piss and got a good
          hiding, end of.

Sammy licks the card and gives it to Marcus. Sammy
then takes the tube from Marcus and snorts a line.

                    MARCUS
        (Wiping the card then putting into his wallet)
          We could have given him more time to pay…

                    SAMMY
                (Cutting in)
          What and let everyone think we're pussies?
          Fuck that.

                    MARCUS
              (Taking the mirror and tube)
          Yeah, fuck it, he'll be alright anyway.

Marcus snorts his line, then puts the mirror into
the glove box and closes it.

                    SAMMY
          *(Wiping his nose and checking it
             in the rearview mirror)*
     Listen, if you don't give one of these
     little skags a pasting every now and then,
     people think you've gone soft. I my friend,
     have got a reputation to build.

                    MARCUS
     All his brothers have turned up though…

                    SAMMY
                (Cutting in)
     And done what? Fuck all, they shit
     themselves when they saw us lot.

They grin at one another, as the car door suddenly
opens on the driver's side. The INTERIOR LIGHT comes
on.

                    RONNIE
          (Putting his head into the car)
     Up you go Sam, there's a good boy.

The lads look startled.

                    RONNIE
               (Turning to Marcus)
     Nine thirty, don't be late.

Ronnie doesn't wait for a reply, he stands out of
frame and firmly shuts the door. In the background,
we see Ronnie walk up the GRAVEL DRIVEWAY to the
house.

Sammy and Marcus sit there aghast.

                    SAMMY
             (Getting out of the motor)
     Fuck me that was close.

                    MARCUS
               (Starting the car)
     He didn't see fuck all mate, don't worry.
     I'll See you in the morning.

Sammy opens the door, smiles at Marcus then jogs up
the driveway after Ronnie.

As Sammy leaves frame, we slowly pan to a car across the street in total darkness. As Ronnie and Sammy enter the house the car's headlights go on, the engine starts and it exit's frame.

18   INT. THE NELSON'S HOUSE – NIGHT.   18

Vince leaves the lights off as he looks around. The house is SOFTLY LIT BY THE MOONLIGHT AND THE STREETLIGHTS. We follow Vince as he slowly walks through to the kitchen and flicks the switch on the KETTLE. He turns to the table and sees a small piece of scrap paper folded in half with George's name on. Vince slowly picks up the note and opens it, the handwritten note reads 'Money's in the jar, Jack x'

CU VINCE'S FACE.

NIGHT SILHOUETTED - Camera swiftly 360s around Vince

F/B.

CU VINCE'S FACE.

DAY/INT - As the camera settles we see Vince but now as a sixteen-year-old boy. The camera pull's back slowly to reveal the exact same place but now in 1984. VINCE IS IN A DREAM LIKE STATE AND VISIBLY STUNNED.

Vince still has the note in his hand, but now it reads 'Take £5 from the pot and get some chips for the boys, love Dad'. Vince flips the note back in half, and on the front is George's name, he then drops it back onto the kitchen table. Vince looks around the kitchen mesmerised, we start to hear cackling children softly getting louder in the background, and it is just as it was all those years ago. TWO CHILDREN RUN QUICKLY PAST VINCE, brushing past him, they startle him.

> YOUNG VINCE
> *(Under his breath)*

Jack?

YOUNG JACK
(*Chasing a slightly older boy*)
Give it back, (turning to Vince) tell him
please Vince, he's got the chain Mum gave
me.

YOUNG VINCE
(*Still stunned*)
Err give it back Bill, and err stop teasing
him.

Vince is overwhelmed that his interaction is so
real. We hear the front door open then close.

DAD NELSON
(*Calling from the other room*)
I'm back boys. Can someone take little
Freddie for me?

A dumbfounded Vince stops a moment it's his father
he loves so dearly, this is all becoming so real, a
chance to see his Dad again.

YOUNG VINCE
(*Trying to speak out loud but unable to do so*)
I'm here Dad.

It's like he has lost the ability to speak, Vince
starts to walk towards the door that is slightly
ajar.

CU - THE NOISE OF THE KETTLE GETS LOUDER AS IT COMES
TO THE BOIL, the switch flips up, it's boiled. It
captures Vince's attention, he turns suddenly to
look at it.

CU VINCE'S FACE.

The camera swiftly 360's around Vince.

CU VINCE'S FACE.

PRESENT DAY.

As the camera settles, we slowly pull back to reveal
that Vince is now back in reality, he is looking at
the steam coming from the kettle that is silhouetted
in the moonlight. He shakes his head in disbelief

and rubs his eyes. He then pulls a packet of herbal
tea from his bag whilst nervously looking around. He
opens the packet and starts to mix it into a cup he
has taken from the draining board with the boiling
water from the kettle. Vince walks through the
kitchen door with the cup of boiling tea in his hand
and enters the front room. He looks around and turns
to look at the sofa.

CU VINCE'S FACE.

NIGHT SILHOUETTED - Again the camera swiftly 360's
around him.

F/B.

CU VINCE'S FACE.

DAY/INT - As the camera settles again on the sixteen
year old Vince, we pull back and pan across to
reveal that we are back in 1984, this time Freddie
is in a bouncer chair. Vince cautiously walks
towards him.

                    VINCE
          (A bit confused, under his breath)
      Well this is strange.

                 DAD NELSON
(Walking into the room with a towel over his shoulder)
      What's strange?

Vince turns and see's his Father, Dad Nelson walks
over to Freddie and picks him up.

                 DAD NELSON (CONT'D)
          (Looking at a visibly stunned Vince)
      Don't you spill that on the carpet. Are you
      alright?

                 YOUNG VINCE
          (Trying to get his words out)
      Err, yeah, err, I mean, err yeah.

Vince and his Father stand looking at each other,
both slightly puzzled.

CU VINCE'S FACE.

                    YOUNG VINCE
(In awe, with a tear in his eye, stumbling over his words)
        I (pause)…

He is interrupted. We hear the door opens in the
kitchen.

CU VINCE'S FACE.

                    FREDDIE (V.O.)
        (Calling) Hello.

As the light comes on Freddie walks around the door,
followed by Jack, we are BACK IN REALITY. Vince
turns and faces them. He puts his tea down on the
dining table.

                    VINCE
          (Wiping a slight tear from his eye)
        Alright boys?

The boys look elated and rush to greet him.

                    JACK
          (Smiling, cuddling Vince)
        Welcome home my brother.

Freddie bashfully waits his turn. Vince pulls him in
to the embrace.

Billy, Frank and George come around the door.

                    JACK (CONT'D)
          (Turning to face them)
        Look, we've got a visitor.

They rush over and greet him.

                    GEORGE
        How was the journey?

                    VINCE
        Long, how's Danny?

                    FRANK
        They said he's gonna be fine.

                    VINCE
     Who's gonna tell me what happened then?

                   GEORGE
        (With the expression on his face changing)
     What the fuck is that smell?

The boys all sniff and look around confused.

                    JACK
                 (Sniffing)
     It smells like flowers. Flowers and shit.

Vince picks his cup up from the table and wafts it
under George's nose.

                    VINCE
     Is it this?

                   GEORGE
        (Turning away holding his nose)
     Yes it fucking well is.

                    VINCE
                 (Smirking)
     Sorry boys it's my herbal tea, it's good
     for the body.

                   GEORGE
     Not so good for the nose though is it.

Freddie and Jack bring some chairs in from the
kitchen.

                    JACK
     I bet the place has changed a lot from the
     last time you saw it?

                    VINCE
            (Looking around confused)
     Yeah, sort of.

Vince is thinking of the surreal experience he had
just had.

GEORGE
(Offering Vince the comfortable chair)
Come and sit here Vince, and we'll tell you
what we know.

19   **INT. SAMMY KEPPEL'S BEDROOM – NIGHT.**   19

Sammy walks around his LAVISH BEDROOM on the phone.

SAMMY
(Cocky)
Give him the three ounces and make sure you
proper bosh 'em (pause) Well fuck him
(pause) Look give it to him now and if he
ain't paid by Wednesday then he gets what
the other geezer got. (Pause) Who wanted
the other two bags? (Pause) Does he have
the money now? (Pause) Bring it to me in
the morning, speak to ya later, bye.
Sammy hangs up, throws his phone on the bed
and turns his stereo up (GRIME) then puts a
LINE OF COKE out on the side. THE DOOR
OPENS, it's his Mother.

LUCY KEPPEL
(Looking around the room)
Come on Sam it's late, turn that down.

SAMMY
(Covering the line of coke with a towel)
Sorry Mum.

Sammy turns the music down.

LUCY KEPPEL
(Smiling)
Thank you darling, good night.

SAMMY
(Blowing her a kiss like butter wouldn't melt)
Night Mum.

As she closes the door, Sammy uncovers the line of
cocaine, straightens it out and snorts it. He throws
his head back and shudders.

20   INT/EXT. JACK'S BEDROOM/CAR/HOSPITAL ENTRANCE, MORNING 20

CU on Jack as he sleeps, he stirs, screws his face
up then inhales.

                         JACK
                      (To himself)
          What is that?

He lifts the covers and sniffs. He then waves his
hand in front of his face indicating a foul odor. He
gets up and opens the bedroom door, walks down to
the kitchen. Vince is there in his jeans and vest
making herbal tea. We can see that Vince has a very
well defined body for a man of his age.

                         JACK
               (Looking at Vince's muscular shape)
          Fuck me Vince. Have you been pumping iron?

                         VINCE
               (Looking around to Jack nonchalantly)
          I live in Thailand Jack, I've been pumping
          everything. You want tea?

                         JACK
               (Screwing his face up again)
          If you mean shit in a cup, then (sarcastic
          smile) no thanks bro.

                         VINCE
                  (Turning to face Jack)
          What time are we going to the hospital?

                         JACK
        (Picking up a piece of Vince's toast as he walks past)
          I'll get ready now.

                         VINCE
          (Taking his vest off and putting his T-shirt on)
          What time did the others leave?

                         JACK
                  (Getting up to get ready)
          How the fuck do I know, you woke me up when
          you poured yourself a cup of ty-Poo.

The camera follows Jack up to the bathroom where he
starts to brush his teeth, Vince follows.

                    JACK
              (Through the toothbrush)
What are you gonna do if you find out what
happened to Danny?

                    VINCE
       (Looking in the mirror over Jacks shoulder)
You mean when I find out what happened to
Danny.

                    JACK
          (Swilling his mouth with water)
Things have changed around here Vince.
People ain't the same as they used to be.

                    VINCE
             (Putting deodorant on)
If they bleed, they talk, simple.

                    JACK
         (Looking admiringly at his brother)
Yeah, I suppose you're right.

They walk down stairs, Vince heads to the front door
as Jack heads toward the back door.

                 JACK (CONT'D)
                  (Smiling)
Oi, where you going?

                    VINCE
        (Turning, as Jack opens the back door)
You got a motor out in the garage?

                    JACK
              (Proud of himself)
Not A motor, the motor.

They walk to the end of the garden. Jack opens the
garage to reveal a mint condition beige V8 3500
Rover with a black vinyl roof.

                    VINCE
                  (Stunned)
Dad's old car!

                         JACK
(Running his hand along the front driver side panel)
         I had her restored, she's like brand new.

The two of them take a moment to admire the car.

HIGH WIDE SHOT - Jack locks up the garage and they
start their journey. As they pull out of the end of
the road, we see a car start up and follow them.

                        VINCE
          (Looking around the car impressed)
         You've restored the lot.

                         JACK
                       (Proud)
         Yeah, it's a piece of Dad, if that makes
         sense.

                        VINCE
                      (Nodding)
         Yeah, it makes perfect sense.

They head toward the hospital. Jack puts the stereo
on.
                         JACK
              (Playing with the stereo)
         The only modern edition is the CD changer
         in the boot.

He puts on an old classic from the seventies, this
triggers some old memories for Vince. Vince starts
to run his finger across the leather on the dash.

CU VINCE

The camera swiftly 360's around him.

F/B.

CU VINCE.

We pull back to reveal Vince continuing to run his
finger across the dash. This time we have gone back
to 1975, the car is still in motion. Dad Nelson is
in the driver's seat with big side burns, a floral
shirt and shades.

                    DAD NELSON
            (Continuing a conversation)
     That's a good question son.

                      VINCE
                    (Dazed)
     What?

                    DAD NELSON
        (Looking down at a seven year old Vince)
     You said what's leather made of. My reply
     to that is (pause) ask your Mother later.

Dad Nelson winks, CU Vince just staring at his
Father in awe.

                    JACK (V.O.)
     You alright?

The camera swiftly 360's around Vince.

PRESENT DAY.

Pull back, Vince shakes his head trying to regain
focus. He looks at a concerned Jack.

                      JACK
                   (Frowning)
     You ok?

                      VINCE
                (Rubbing his eyes)
     Yeah, a bit jet lagged I think.

They park the car in the hospital car park, exit the
car and walk in to the entrance of the hospital.

                      JACK
          (Looking at two nurses and smiling)
     Alright ladies?

Vince shakes his head and laughs as the nurses
ignore Jack.

                   JACK (CONT'D)
                (Turning to Vince)
     What about you Vince? You got anyone
     special in your life?

                    VINCE
          (Without batting an eyelid)
     Yeah, me.

                    JACK
     Wait here a minute, I've got to have a
     piss.

Jack walks into the toilet while Vince waits
outside.

21   INT/EXT. PATTERSON'S CAR, HOSPITAL CAR PARK – DAY.   21

Vince is inside the hospital waiting for Jack.

                 DI PATTERSON
             (Almost to himself)
     Well well well, Vince Nelson.

                 DS DELGADO
     Another one of the brothers? How many has
     he got?

Patterson glances at Delgado then looks back at
Vince.

                 DI PATTERSON
             (Ignoring the question)
     This one is different. Me and this one have
     got a bit of history (under his breath)
     this could get very interesting.

                 DS DELGADO
     Are we going to question them now or…

Jack exits the toilet, Vince and Jack walk out of
sight.

                 DI PATTERSON
         (Cutting in and starting the engine)
     No, later.

They pull out of the car park hastily.

22   **INT. HOSPITAL BED – DAY.**   22

George sits holding Danny's hand, Freddie is reading
a magazine and Billy is asleep in the chair. We see
Jack and Vince walk into the room.

> GEORGE
> *(Sitting up)*
Hello lads.

> VINCE
> *(Putting his hand on George's shoulder)*
Why didn't you wake me up?

> GEORGE
> *(Caring)*
You needed to sleep after your journey.

George makes way so Vince can sit down.

> VINCE
> *(Looking at Danny)*
Hello mate, I got here as quick as I could.

A motionless Danny lies in the bed, still in the
same condition. Billy wakes up.

> VINCE
> *(Looking at George)*
Where was he stabbed?

> GEORGE
> *(Indicating on his own body)*
Twice under his arm, once near his kidney,
and five times on the top of his right leg.

Vince grits his teeth and shaking his head.

> BILLY
> *(Stern)*
It's got to be sorted Vince.

> VINCE
> *(Nodding)*
It will be.

A nurse enters and approaches George.

                    NURSE
                (Talking gently)
Mr. Nelson the specialist would like to see
Danny, and has asked if we could minimize
the amount of people in the room, (looking
around at the brothers) sorry guys.

                   GEORGE
                 (Maturely)
No problem love, can you give us ten
minutes.

The nurse nods, smiles then exits quietly.

              GEORGE (CONT'D)
               (To the group)
I want to stay, what do you think?

                    JACK
                 (Agreeing)
No problem mate, I can get us back (looking
around the room).

                   BILLY
                (Getting up)
Drop me at the pub then Jack.

                  FREDDIE
            (Pulling out his mobile)
I'll give Frank a bell and tell him to wait
for a call.

                    JACK
                (To Freddie)
Then you can come home with me and sort
that washing out.

                   VINCE
                (To George)
I'll stop with you for a while.

One by one Jack, Freddie and Billy kiss Danny on the
forehead then exit. George and Vince are alone with
Danny.

                    GEORGE
        (Holding Danny's hand, looking at Vince)
Whatever happens, I don't want any more
trouble on my doorstep.

                    VINCE
                (Stern)
I can't promise that George.

                    GEORGE
        (Upset, with a tear in his eye)
Look at him, just look at him Vince.

Vince looks down at his little brother who is laying
there helpless. Vince grits his teeth again.

                GEORGE (CONT'D)
                (Caring)
I don't want anyone else to get hurt.

                    VINCE
That's why I'm here, to stop it all.

                    GEORGE
                (Upset)
What are you gonna do Vince? Trouble seems
to follows you wherever you go. (Pause) I
mean it. I don't want any of them getting
hurt. What's done is done and we've got to
let the police deal with it now.

                    VINCE
            (Slightly put out)
Fuck that, it's my family and I deal with
it.

Vince gets up and slowly walks toward the door.

                    GEORGE
            (Looking at Vince)
Where you been then for the last twenty
years Vince? Who the fuck do you think was
protecting them all that time? Who the fuck
do you think will protect them when you go
again?

Vince opens the door and looks back at George.

                    VINCE
     I'm grateful for everything you've done for
     them George, I truly mean that. But, we've
     got different ways of dealing with things
     and you know how I get things done.

He takes a step through the door.

                    GEORGE
     Don't get the others involved in anything,
     I mean it.

Vince pauses then turns to face George.

                    VINCE
                (Reassuring smile)
     I'll do it alone you have my word.

                    GEORGE
                (Soft smile)
     Make sure you do Vince.

They exchange a knowing look for a beat. Vince winks
as he starts to close the door.

                    VINCE (V.O.)
     Time to let people know I'm home.

As Vince leaves, George sits with Danny alone.
HIGH WIDE SHOT - hospital entrance (music softly
starts). Vince walks out of the hospital, stops for
a beat to flip his collar up, and then walks on
ready for business. We watch him walk off into the
distance.

CREDITS ROLL.

REFLECTION: CLOSING MONOLOGUE

So, there you have it, the Nelson boys. Dysfunctional? Yeah probably, but then again, who's family isn't? I have truly missed them, that's for sure and being with them again has shown me that. I'll tell you one thing I haven't missed, the bits around the edges, the demons. It's taken me a long time to battle with these, a long time for those scars to heal. But it's all becoming clearer, much clearer. Ronnie and Lenny, two of the best friends I had ever had, Ronnie, I respected very, very much growing up. Not anymore. Lenny is the result of the choices he has made, a life of empty dreams. As for DI Patterson, like he said, we've got a bit of history. Can't help thinking that business with him is not concluded, we'll have to see. Time certainly makes things easier, but they don't help you forget. Now this, poor Danny, I love him so much. He's one of the nicest and most honest people I've ever known. Things will be sorted and I will definitely be there when they need me. It will be emotional, there will be confrontation and people will definitely get hurt. One thing is for sure, there's only one man I fear in this world, and that's me.

FADE TO BLACK.

END OF EPISODE 1.

47

Episode 2

Danny boy

INTRODUCTION: OPENING MONOLOGUE

It looks like things have to be dealt with, I know George wants an amicable resolve, but people like me just don't do things that way. It seems like these people have forgotten the true value of what it's like to be in things together, to be part of a community. Drugs and the people who sell them have destroyed this place, this council estate now just oozes poverty and depression. People just want to get on with life, as boring as it may seem, but nonetheless people just want to be left alone. Then you've got the other side of the fence, the people who want to run things, the people who think they are untouchable, the big dogs, the lords of this so-called manor. Well, it's time they knew I was back. I can't say I've never lost a fight, but I can say one thing, I've learnt every time I have. That's what has made me strong, I'm not talking about physically, I'm talking about mentally, I'm talking about mind-set. Someone has done something to disrespect my family and it can be dealt with in one of two ways. Amicably or with prejudice and the way forward will not depend on what I do, it will depend on the reactions of others to the things I do. Either way, it's no problem for me, no problem at all.

It is not only what we do that we are held responsible, but also for what we do not do - Moliere

1   **EXT. THE MOON PUB – DAY.**   1

EPISODE 2 - Danny boy.

CREDITS ROLL - TITLE MUSIC.

AS THE CAMERA SLOWLY PANS ACROSS THE BAR - we see
Lenny serving, the place is quiet with SOFT MUSIC
PLAYING, and Billy is sitting at the bar with a
drink in his hand. Sammy Keppel is playing pool in
the background with a few friends.

END OF CREDITS.

AS THE CAMERA PANS ACROSS THE BAR, WE FOCUS ON LENNY
IN THE FOREGROUND AND FREEZE WHILE VINCE NARRATES.

                    VINCE (V.O.)
        That's Lenny Hodge, me him and Ronnie
        Keppel were inseparable once upon a time.
        Lenny's a proper diamond, a truer friend
        you will never find, I mean that. I've
        always trusted him, and I always will.

UNFREEZE. WE SEE VINCE ENTER OTS IN THE BACKGROUND -
he slowly walks toward Billy and Lenny in the
foreground.

                      VINCE
          (Slowly approaching Lenny)
        Barman, get me a light and bitter, make it
        quick I'm in a rush.

Lenny frowns as if he recognizes the voice then
turns to see Vince.

                      LENNY
      (Smiling, making his way around the bar)
        Vince, you old bastard.

He embraces a ridged, slightly taken back Vince.

                  LENNY (CONT'D)
              (Elated)
        It's really you, it's great to see you
        mate, what brings you here after all this
        time?

                    VINCE
          (Sincere and stern, looking directly at Lenny)
          I've come to right a few wrongs.

                    LENNY
                  (Falling in)
          Oh, yeah, I'm sorry to hear about Danny.

                    VINCE
            (Putting a hand on Lenny's shoulder)
          Thanks Len.

                    LENNY
               (Reflecting on the past)
          Why didn't you contact me or come back once
          in a while?

                    VINCE
            (Looking away, then looking around)
          Nah, I wanted a clean break. I needed to
          start over, somewhere different. Too many
          bad memories here.

Vince and Lenny embrace again. Billy smiles as Sammy
looks on curiously from the background.

                    LENNY
               (Handing over the drink)
          I can't believe it. Vince Nelson in the
          flesh. You do know that nobody drinks this
          shit any more don't ya?

                    VINCE
            *(Giving the place the once over, then
                noticing the CCTV cameras)*
          This place ain't changed.

                    LENNY
               (Walking back behind the bar)
          Yeah, well Ronnie owns it now.

Lenny moves into the foreground, now facing
camera,OTS, Vince also facing camera in the
background.

FOCUS ON VINCE.

                    VINCE
          (Slowly taking a seat next to Billy)
        Is that right. How is he?

FOCUS SHIFTS ONTO LENNY.

                    LENNY
     (Looking sheepish, Sammy looks on curiously)
        Yeah, he's fine.

FOCUS SLOWLY SHIFTS ONTO VINCE.

                    VINCE
                  (Vigilantly)
        And Lucy?

QUICK FOCUS SHIFT ONTO LENNY.

                    LENNY
   (Pausing a moment, looking at Sammy then answering)
         She's fine too.

The awkward silence is broken by Billy belching. Billy
Pulls a ten pound note out of his pocket and offers
his glass to Lenny.

                    BILLY
        One more in here as well please Len.

                    LENNY
          (Pulling the pint, looking at Vince)
        Sure mate, no problem.

Without breaking eye contact, Vince Pushes the money
back towards Billy.

                    VINCE
                (Stern and cool)
        These ones will be on the house. You know
        for old time sake and all that bollocks.

                    LENNY
          (Looking around to see if Sammy's looking)
        Ronnie will shoot me if he finds out.

Lenny smirks deviously and puts the drinks on the
bar.

                    VINCE
             (Smiling back at him)
         I'll fucking shoot you if you don't!

They exchange a wry smile and chink their glasses
ready to reminisce.

TIME SKIP - catching up, drinking, talking and
laughing.

                    LENNY
             (Enjoying the company)
         Bloody hell I can't believe that, so after
         the nine stretch you went up north.

                    VINCE
             (Letting his guard down slightly)
         Yeah, I was cell'd up with this bloke from
         Leeds called Dave. We got on like a house
         on fire. Ironic really, he was doing a five
         for arson.

                    LENNY
             (Smiling)
         So you went to Leeds then?

                    VINCE
         Yeah, his brother put us up for a while,
         and we got a job working the door at this
         shitty little club run by the local Tony
         Montana. He was a right little two bob
         wanker.

                    LENNY
             (Shaking his head with a grin on his face)
         How long then?

                    VINCE
             (With a wry smile)
         How long what?

                    LENNY
             (Smiling)
         How long before you stuck it on him?

                    VINCE
                 (Falling in)
Oh. Two months, then we had to fuck off a
bit sharpish. Not before Dave took ten
grand from the geezer's safe mind you. You
know the saying Len, when life gives you
lemons.
                    LENNY
                 (Smiling)
So this gangster bloke, did he come after
you then?

                    VINCE
Nah that was the beauty of it. After we
turned him over, the fella he worked for
didn't trust him any more so he put Dave's
brother in charge of business. So me and
Dave fucked off to Thailand and opened a
bar everything was hunky-dory.

Sammy appears in frame, at the bar next to Billy.

                    SAMMY
                 (Cocky to Lenny)
Get me a beer.

Turning to face Billy and Vince.

                    SAMMY
    (Offering his hand to them as a gesture)
I'm Sammy.

Billy looks at it then drains his glass. Vince feels
slightly uncomfortable for the lad and shakes his
hand.

                    VINCE
                 (Calmly)
    I'm Vince.

                    LENNY
             (Putting the drinks on the bar)
There you go Sammy.

Sammy doesn't even acknowledge him.

VINCE
(To Lenny, not breaking eye contact with Sammy)
I'll get that.

LENNY
(Nervously)
No, it's ok Vince, Sammy don't pay for
drinks.

SAMMY
(Cutting in smug)
My Dad's pub see.

VINCE
(Realising who Sammy is)
Oh right.

SAMMY
(Curious and to the point)
How do you know Lenny then?

VINCE
(Coolly sipping his drink)
Me and Len, we go way back.

SAMMY
(Abrupt)
You must know my Dad then?

VINCE
(Knowing smile)
Yeah. I know your Dad.

Sammy is now full of confidence.

SAMMY
(Brash)
Well if you get any trouble in here just
give me a shout. Nice to meet you mate.

VINCE
(Offering an obligatory nod)
Yeah, you too Sammy.

Vince and Billy watch Sammy return to the pool
table.

                    BILLY
              (Swigging his drink)
     That is one smug little wanker.

                    VINCE
           (Looking at Sammy curiously)
     I'll keep him sweet for now I think, he
     might come in handy.

Vince drains his pint and gets up to leave.

                 VINCE (CONT'D)
              (Putting his coat on)
     Drink up Bill, we're going into town to get
     George some grub.

Billy looks narked that he has to leave the pub, but
follows Vince.

                    LENNY
                 (Candidly)
     Good luck with your brother Vince, send him
     my kindest regards.

                    VINCE
           (Pointing at Lenny and winking)
     I'll be back in to see you later Len. Be
     good.

As they leave Vince bumps into Marcus in the doorway
as Marcus is entering the pub.

                    VINCE
      (Casually glancing back at Marcus and carrying on)
        Sorry mate.

Marcus looks a bit taken back as Vince and Billy
brush him aside. He walks over to meet Sammy just as
Sammy gets to the bar.

                    SAMMY
                 (Questioning)
     That geezer Vince, is that Danny's brother
     from Thailand?

                    LENNY
              (A bit more confident)
     Yep, it certainly is.

Lenny wipes the side. SAMMY GRABS HIS ARM FIRMLY.

                    SAMMY
             (Through gritted teeth)
He thinks he's a bit of a face don't he?

                    LENNY
(Pulling his arm away from Sammy grasp and frowning)
     Not really. He's just here to find out what
     happened to Danny, that's all.

                    MARCUS
                   (Cocky)
     He'll end up in the same place as his
     brother if he pushes past me like that
     again.

Lenny smirks to himself.

                    SAMMY
                 (To Lenny)
     Go on, what's so funny?

                    LENNY
             (Feeling the pressure)
     Nah, Nothing.

                    MARCUS
             (Grabbing Lenny's collar)
     Go on Len, you can tell us. What's so
     amusing?

                    LENNY
      (Pulling his shirt out of Marcus's grip)
     Alright, alright.

Lenny leans across the bar to face Sammy and Marcus.

                    LENNY (CONT'D)
                  (Firmly)
     If you want to put Vince Nelson into
     hospital, you'd better run him over with a
     truck. And let me tell you one thing, if
     you do that, make sure you've got your
     seatbelt on.

                    SAMMY
                (Unimpressed)
        So he does think he's a face?

                    LENNY
    (Walking to the other side of the bar and calling back)
            Ask your Dad.

2   **INT/EXT. POLICE STATION - DAY**   2

Patterson is on the phone. Delgado is on his
computer, but we can see that he is fully aware of
Patterson's phone call.

                    PATTERSON
        (Pacing around his desk, talking into his phone)
        I've seen him with my own two eyes…

The person on the phone cuts Patterson short.

                PATTERSON (CONT'D)
                (Flustered)
        We need to meet and discuss what we do now.

Patterson raises his voice slightly and turns his
back to Delgado.

                PATTERSON (CONT'D)
            (Concerned and at volume)
        That's easy for you to say but I've…

Swiftly, Patterson is cut short again.

                    PATTERSON
                (Apologetic)
        Sorry. I'm sorry alright. I don't mean to
        shout, but it's just that I'm a little
        concerned at…

Patterson, again cut short. He is forced to listen
intently.

                    PATTERSON
                (Slightly calmer)
        Ok. Will do.

Patterson hangs up the phone and stares thoughtfully
out of the window for a moment. He swiftly turns, as

he does so Delgado quickly looks the other way as if
he had not heard any of Patterson's conversation.

                    PATTERSON
                  (A bit shaken)
      I'm popping out for a while.

                    DELGADO
                 (About to stand)
      Shall I come with you?

                    PATTERSON
                     (Firm)
      No, no it's fine. I'll call in later.

Delgado watches Patterson leave then picks up the
phone to dial a number.

3   INT. HOSPITAL BED – DAY   3

George is by Danny's side as Vince and Billy arrive.
George is asleep with his head on the edge of
Danny's bed. Billy slowly opens the door. George
sleepily looks up.

                    GEORGE
          (Yawning and rubbing his eyes)
      Alright?

                    BILLY
               (Handing him a bag)
      We got you a couple of rolls.

                    GEORGE
             (Looking at Billy and Vince)
      Cheers.

                    VINCE
               (Holding Danny's hand)
      So what did the specialist say?

                    GEORGE
   (Pulling a roll from the bag and taking a bite)
      To just be patient really, he's stable at
      the moment, but they still need to look at
      the bruising on his chest. The Doctor also
      looked a bit concerned when he changed the
      dressing on his head.

                    VINCE
                 (Frowning)
Why, what do you mean?

                    GEORGE
                 (Sincere)
It's a big wound Vince, the Doctor called
the specialist out of the room to talk. I
couldn't really hear what they said.

                    VINCE
             (Slightly narked)
You never asked what was up?

                    GEORGE
        (Turning his attention back to Danny)
If it was that important they would have
said something there and then.

Frank enters in his work clothes.

                    FRANK
          (Acknowledging the brothers)
How is he?

                    GEORGE
             (Tired of saying it)
Same.

Frank takes a seat.

                    BILLY
             (Making small talk)
How was work Frank?

                    FRANK
             (Getting comfortable)
Yeah good, I just finished. My last job was
just around the corner.

                    GEORGE
                 (Caring)
Have you been home yet?

                    FRANK
          (Sitting back in the chair)
Not yet mate I came straight here. I rang
Jo and told her I'll be late.

                    VINCE
          (Remembering to ask after Frank's family)
Oh. How are Jo and the girls?

                    FRANK
          (Pleased he had asked)
Yeah, great. They're looking forward to
seeing you at some point. You ain't seen
the girls since they were babies.

                    VINCE
               (Smiling)
How old are they now?

                    FRANK
               (Proudly)
Chloe's nine now, and Jesse is eight.

                    GEORGE
          (Annoyed at all the talking)
Frank you may as well go home mate, there's
nothing you can do here.

George looks over at Vince and Billy.

                GEORGE (CONT'D)
          (Signally for them to go too)
And you two. I'll give you a bell if
anything changes.

                    BILLY
          (Getting to his feet)
Righto mate, Frank you going past the
boozer?

Frank and Billy carry on their conversation.

                    VINCE
            (Quietly to George)
What about you? You need to rest too, have
a bath, and change your clothes or
something.

                    GEORGE
          (Looking down at Danny)
It's alright, Jack's on his way down with
my stuff. Anyway, they said I can use the

shower here, and they're gonna bring a camp
bed in for me to sleep on.

                    VINCE
                 (Surprised)
You're staying all night?

                    GEORGE
                  (Thrown)
Yeah well I can't leave him like this, all
on his own. It's what Dad would have done
for any of us lot. I'll call you if
anything changes.

                    VINCE
              (Reassuring smile)
Ok mate.

As Vince turns to walk away, George pulls him back.

                    GEORGE
                 (Quietly)
It's good to have you home Vince. I really
mean that.

George and Vince embrace. Finally, George feels like
there is someone there for him.

4   **INT. KEPPEL'S HOUSE - DAY**   4

Lucy is making a sandwich. Sammy sits at the
breakfast bar.

                    SAMMY
                (Inpatient)
Come on Mum, I'm starving.

                    LUCY
               (Ignoring him)
Are you in for dinner tonight?

                    SAMMY
           (Flicking through a mag)
Dunno yet.

Sammy suddenly remembers his encounter with Vince.

                    SAMMY (CONT'D)
                   (Inquisitively)
Mum, do you know a geezer called Vince
Nelson?

Lucy fumbles with what she is doing and drops the
knife.

                         LUCY
 (Picking the knife up and pulling herself together)
     What? Who? Vince Nelson?

                        SAMMY
      (Looking at her worryingly puzzled)
Err yeah, Vince Nelson. You alright Mum you
look like you've seen a ghost?

                         LUCY
            (Collecting herself)
Yeah, I'm fine. Vince Nelson, yeah, name
rings a bell.

Ronnie walks in putting his tie on.

                   LUCY (CONT'D)
         (Quickly changing the subject)
Do you want salad cream on this love?

                        SAMMY
(Turning his attention to Ronnie, answering his mum)
Yeah. Dad I met a bloke at lunchtime who
reckons he knows you. Vince Nelson.

                        RONNIE
               (Clearly startled)
What? Where was he? Vince Nelson, are you
sure?

                        SAMMY
             (Curiously confused)
Yeah, positive. Stocky bloke, about your
age or a bit younger.

                        RONNIE
(Looking at Lucy, slightly angered, slightly scared)
     What did he say to you?

Sammy tucks into his sandwich nonchalantly.

                    SAMMY
              (*Playing it cool*)
     Nothing really.

                    RONNIE
(*Grabbing Sammy's wrists and slightly raising his voice*)
     Don't fuck me about Son. What did he say?

                    SAMMY
              (*Taken back*)
     Nothing. What's wrong with you?

                    RONNIE
            (*Letting go of Sammy*)
     Nothing son, I'm sorry alright.

Ronnie composes himself for a moment.

                RONNIE (CONT'D)
              (*Tying to be calm*)
     It's just, Vince is an old friend of mine,
     and he's a very dangerous bloke. Don't go
     near him alright. I mean that Sammy, stay
     away from that man at all costs.

                    SAMMY
                 (*Cocky*)
     Don't worry about me Dad, I've got Marcus.

                    RONNIE
            (*Raising his voice again*)
     Fuck Marcus. Vince is in a different
     league. Give me your word. I fucking mean
     it.

                    SAMMY
               (*Concerned*)
     Ok Dad, I promise.

Sammy gets up and slowly starts to walk upstairs.

                    SAMMY
               (*Turning back*)
     Lenny said he was an 'ard nut.

Sammy carries on walking. Lucy and Ronnie watch him
leave.

                         RONNIE
          That's all I fucking need.
          (Slowly turning to Lucy)
          That goes for you as well.

                         LUCY
                     (Confused)
          What does?

Ronnie picks his mobile up and starts walking out.
He turns back as he opens the door.

                         RONNIE
                    (Pointing)
          Stay the fuck away from him.

He exits and shuts the door firmly.

5   EXT. BRICKYARD – DAY.   5

HIGH WIDE SHOT - Patterson is standing alone in a
derelict brickyard, isolated but cautious about who
he is about to meet. He turns to see a BENTLEY
pulling into the yard, leaving a trail of dust as it
heads towards Patterson's lone figure.

LOW WIDE SHOT – car stops, dirty foreground of tire,
looking along the side of the shiny car. The door
opens and a WELL-POLISHED ITALIAN LEATHER SHOE drops
into frame onto the gravel. We can hear the gravel
crunch as Charlie Madigan gets out and shuts the
door behind him. The camera slowly jibs up and
settles on a CU of Charlie who lights a cigar before
turning to face Patterson who is now OTS.

                         CHARLIE
                (Cool and in control)
          I pay arseholes like you not to panic.

Charlie slowly walks around behind Patterson looking
at the WIDE-OPEN SPACE they are now in.

                         PATTERSON
          (Worried, turning to look at Charlie)
          Sorry Charlie but I'm worried.

CHARLIE
(Still not making eye contact)
So he's back? And what?

PATTERSON
(Reiterating)
We put an innocent man behind bars…

CHARLIE
(Cutting in conceitedly)
Shit like that happens all the time. Ronnie stole my daughter off him and we killed his Dad, but all that was a long long time ago. He's only back to find out what happened to his brother. I doubt he'll even give all that shit a second thought after all this time.

Charlie slowly walks around Patterson again making him feel uneasy.

PATTERSON
(Still concerned)
If anyone blabs then we…

CHARLIE
(Cool cutting in again)
Relax. Just fucking relax. Who's gonna talk? The only other person that knows what went on that night is that fucking div Lenny, and after his part in it all, I'm sure his lips are well and truly sealed.

PATTERSON
(Concerned)
What about Lucy?

CHARLIE
(Angered)
Leave my fucking daughter out of this. She knows nothing, and if she ever finds out what we've done, its me you'll have to worry about.

Charlie's phone rings, he looks to see who it is then answers.

                    CHARLIE
               (Into the phone)
     Hello Ron.

SPLIT SCEREEN - PHONE CONVERSATION.

                    RONNIE
                 (Worried)
     Vince Nelson's back!

                    CHARLIE
                  (Cool)
     Yeah yeah yeah, so I hear. Don't worry,
     it's in hand.

                    RONNIE
              (Still irritated)
     If he starts asking questions…

                    CHARLIE
                (Cutting in)
     He won't.

                    RONNIE
                 (Worried)
     I'm gonna go through the CCTV cameras in
     the bar to see who he's spoken to.

                    CHARLIE
                  (Firm)
     What are you worried about? Just forget it
     for now. If he starts digging, then I'll
     get him dealt with.

Patterson shakes his head in disbelief.

               CHARLIE (CONT'D)
            (Not waiting for a reply)
     Speak to you later.

Charlie hangs up and turns to Patterson. FULL SCREEN

                    PATTERSON
                 (Curious)
     So how are you going to do that then?

Charlie gets into his car and starts it up.

                    CHARLIE
          (*Making eye contact for the first time*)
However I fucking wanna do it. I pay you a
lot of dough to turn a blind eye and keep
quiet, so let's not question who's in
charge.

Charlie looks firmly at an uneasy looking Patterson.

                CHARLIE (CONT'D)
          (*Looking Patterson up and down*)
I'll ring ya.

HIGH WIDE SHOT - Charlie pulls off leaving a cloud
of dust behind him, a solitary Patterson watches him
leave.

6   **INT. HOSPITAL - EVENING.**   6

George is talking to a nurse as Jack arrives. He
sees Jack and finishes his conversation, the nurse
walks off. George walks over to greet Jack who is
holding George's overnight bag.

                    GEORGE
              (*Taking the bag*)
Thanks a lot Jack.

They slowly walk toward Danny's room.

                    JACK
              (*Remembering*)
Oh, I put your Jeans in.

                    GEORGE
            (*Opening the door*)
Nice one Jack.

                    JACK
         (*Moving to Danny's bedside*)
What's been happening here then?

                    GEORGE
              (*Visibly tired*)
Nothing's changed really mate. They're
gonna look at him again in the morning. The
drugs are keeping him comfortable for now.

George starts to unpack his bag.

                    GEORGE
                (Considerate)
    When you leave Jack, do me a favor, keep an
    eye on Vince for me.

                     JACK
                 (Curious)
    Why? What you thinking?

                    GEORGE
             (Shaking his head)
    I've got a feeling he's out to settle a few
    old scores. Just don't let Freddie get
    involved.

7   **INT. THE MOON PUB – EVENING**   7

Lenny wipes the optics and Billy sits at the bar.

                    LENNY
             (Mid-conversation)
    What one, The Dog and Duck or the Mucky
    Duck?

                    BILLY
             (Necking his chaser)
    The Dog and Duck, the barmaid's got great
    big bangers, and a proper cackley laugh.

They laugh as a stern faced Ronnie walks in and
heads to the back of the pub.

                    RONNIE
            (Moving around the bar)
    Len, a word.

A slightly worried Lenny looks at Billy then heads
toward Ronnie.

                    LENNY
             (Slightly scared)
    What's up boss?

Lenny puts his cloth on the bar and starts cleaning
as they speak.

NO PARKING
IN USE DAY +
NIGHT

London Borough of Croydon
No ball games
allowed

                    RONNIE
     (Moving uncomfortably close to Lenny's face)
Anyone been in that I should know about?

                    LENNY
       (Knowing who Ronnie is talking about)
Well I…

                    RONNIE
        (Cutting in, through gritted teeth)
Vince fucking Nelson.

                    LENNY
                (Bumbling)
Oh yeah Vin…

                    RONNIE
      (Squeezing Lenny's hand on the bar)
Why the fuck didn't you call me.

                    LENNY
        (Nervously wincing in pain)
I never had th…

                    RONNIE
(Cutting in, quickly grabbing Lenny's collar)
You tell him anything Len, and I mean
anything, and you're a dead man. Do you
understand?

Ronnie lets go and smiles for show.

                    LENNY
             (Clearly shaken)
Course Guv, you can trust me.

Ronnie exits through a door marked PRIVATE. Billy
sees the exchange but pretends he hasn't, Lenny
picks the cloth up and sheepishly resumes cleaning.

                    BILLY
           (Finishing his pint)
Len, another drink over here for the
thirsty bloke.

Lenny pours Billy a shot and a pint. Freddie walks in
and makes his way over to Billy's side. Billy double
takes, seeing Freddie's new haircut.

                    FREDDIE
                (Looking sharp)
You seen Vince anywhere?

                     BILLY
              (Getting his money out)
Yeah he stopped at Frank's to see the
girls.

Billy points at his drink.

                  BILLY (CONT'D)
 You want one?

                    FREDDIE
                   (Coyly)
Yeah, a light and bitter please.

Billy and Lenny exchange a look.

                     BILLY
                 (Playfully)
Light and bitter, since when?

                    FREDDIE
              (Thinking on his feet)
Err well I fancy a change.

                     BILLY
                  (Smiling)
New haircut?

                    FREDDIE
                    (Cool)
Yeah, it's the new me. I ain't gonna take
shit from anyone from now on, you mark my
words.

Freddie casually leans on the bar.

                     BILLY
                  (Mocking)
That's good mate, get your elbows of the
bar.
                    FREDDIE
              (Standing upright)
Sorry Bill.

                    BILLY
                  (Mocking)
       Yeah, you're an animal kiddo.

Lenny and Billy smile at each other.

                   FREDDIE
                 (Falling in)
        Piss off you two.

They laugh as Vince enters and heads over.

                    VINCE
                (To the group)
       Alright?

                   FREDDIE
                (Admiringly)
       Alright Vince?

                    BILLY
               (Winking at Vince)
       Seen Freddie's new haircut, he reminds me
       of you when you were younger.

                    VINCE
              (Looking flippantly)
       Nice one Freddie.

Freddie is chuffed.

We see Ronnie in the background looking over at Vince,
Freddie and Billy. He looks hateful and scorned.

                   RONNIE
            (Under his breath to himself)
       Well here goes.

He swaggers over confidently.

                RONNIE (CONT'D)
                  (Smooth)
       Vince Nelson, now there's a face I never
       thought I'd see again.

They turn and face Ronnie who has made his way
BEHIND THE BAR to ensure there is SIX FOOT OF
MAHOGANY between them.

An awkward silence ensues, as they look each other
up and down.

> VINCE
> *(Stern)*
> Hello Ron, long time.

They begrudgingly shake hands, and stare one another
in the eye.

> RONNIE
> *(Insincere, chirpy)*
> Too long, how have you been?

Another awkward moment follows.

> VINCE
> *(Smile)*
> Not bad considering. You?

> RONNIE
> *(Breaking eye contact)*
> So so, you know how it is.

> VINCE
> *(Brazenly)*
> How's Lucy?

Another awkward silence.

> RONNIE
> She's fine.

Ronnie squirms and is clearly uncomfortable.

> RONNIE (CONT'D)
> *(Changing the subject)*
> So what brings you back after all this time
> Vince?

Jack enters in the background and moves to join the
brothers at the bar. Lenny starts to pours him a
pint.

The brothers and Lenny watch the standoff in
anticipation.

                     VINCE
                  (Unyielding)
Danny.

                     RONNIE
            (Looking at the brothers)
Sorry to hear about that, the streets just
ain't a safe place anymore are they?

                     VINCE
          (Sternly looking for a reaction)
Someone has taken a liberty with my brother
Ronnie. That's not good news for them I can
assure you of that.

                     RONNIE
            (Knowing what he means)
Well, if I hear of anything I'll give you a
shout.

They look at each other, eye to eye. Ronnie starts
to fidget again but cannot break eye contact.

                 RONNIE (CONT'D)
            (Changing the subject)
You bumped into my boy today I hear?

                     VINCE
                  (Still firm)
Yeah, he seems like a good kid.

                     RONNIE
          (Pausing then slowly nodding)
Yeah, he is. Look, we should have a pint
and catch up on old times.

                     VINCE
                 (Dismissive)
If you say so Ron.

Lenny breaks the uncomfortable silence.

                     LENNY
          (Trying to ease the tension)
It's Sammy's birthday party in the back
room tonight. I suppose you two could catch
up then.

                    RONNIE
     *(Shooting Lenny a look, then turning to
          Vince smiling knowingly)*
What a good idea. Bring your brothers.
Vince, you can come as my guests.

                    VINCE
          (Slightly reactive)
Your guest?

Vince gathers himself.

                    VINCE (CONT'D)
          (Settling down)
I'll see what's happening with Danny first.

Ronnie makes his way toward the back room.

                    RONNIE
     (Cocky, as now he has a wider audience)
Oh come on Vince, I insist.

                    LENNY
          (To Vince quietly)
Lucy'll be there.

                    VINCE
          (Calling out to Ronnie)
I'll be there.

Ronnie opens the door then turns.

                    RONNIE
          (Dramatic)
I look forward to it.

Ronnie exits.

                    JACK
          (Confused)
Tell me we ain't going?

                    VINCE
          (Putting his coat on)
Yeah. We might find something out about
Danny. Drink up you two, let's go home and
get sorted.

Billy shakes his head and downs his pint as the boys get up to go. The Nelson Boys walk toward the door.

> VINCE (CONT'D)
> *(Calling back)*
> See you tonight Len.

The boys say goodbye to Lenny.

> BILLY
> *(As he walks through the door)*
> Can we stop at the Offie?

8   INT. HOSPITAL – EVENING.   8

George is on the phone outside the room.

> GEORGE
> *(Into the phone, pacing)*
> Honestly Vince. I'll call Jack's mobile if anything changes, besides you're nearer to the hospital in the pub than you are at home.

George reassures Vince.

> GEORGE (CONT'D)
> *(Sincerely)*
> I will, see you soon. Bye mate.

He hangs up, walks to the door and looks at Danny.

> GEORGE (CONT'D)
> *(With a tear in his eye)*
> Oh Dan, what did you get yourself into?

9   INT. THE MOON PUB/BACK ROOM – NIGHT.   9

The party is in full swing. The LOCAL BAND is playing SKA MUSIC as the brothers enter. It is packed, but the Nelson boys manage to find a table. As the Nelson boys pass the band, THE SINGER recognises Vince.

> SINGER
> *(Surprised)*
> Vince Nelson wow. Good to see you man.

                    VINCE
        (Smiling back, shaking the singer's hand)
    You're better than I remember.

                    SINGER
            (Smiling, laughing)
    Thanks man, you wanna hear anything
    special?

The singer looks over at Ronnie who looks and points
at his watch sarcastically.

                    VINCE
              (Reminiscently)
    Any of the old ones.

                    SINGER
                (Smiling)
    I've got a special one for ya. You're gonna
    love it Vince.

                    VINCE
          (Walking over to the table)
    Well let's hear it then.

They exchange a knowing smile.

The brothers sit down.

The band start to play an old song that means something
to both Vince and Ronnie.

Vince and Ronnie exchange a glance.

                    VINCE
            (Giving Jack some money)
    Here's a score Jack, get 'em in.

                    JACK
            (Signalling to Freddie)
    Come on Fred.

Vince stands and takes his jacket off to reveal a tight
white T-shirt. Freddie does the same.

Vince looks puzzled as Freddie heads toward the bar
with Jack.

                    BILLY
              (Pointing toward Freddie)
     What? He idolises you mate.

                    VINCE
               (Proud but coy)
     Me, why what have I done?

                    BILLY
               (Enlightening)
     It's your reputation Vince. Let's face it,
     your more like Dad than any of us.

                    VINCE
                (Smiling)
     I'll take that as a compliment.

                    BILLY
         (Smiling back and winking)
     You fucking well should.

Vince looks around the room as a few old faces nod,
smile and acknowledge Vince.

Freddie and Jack put the drinks on the table. Vince
clocks Sammy pointing over at them.

                    VINCE
               (To Freddie)
     Who's that with Sammy Keppel?

                    FREDDIE
              (Turning to look)
     Oh that's Marcus, he's nothing for us to
     worry about.

Billy smirks at Vince.

                    VINCE
              (To all of them)
     Listen, if it kicks off at any time, not that
     it will, but if it does, I want you all to
     stay out of it. Whatever the situation is, I
     can handle it, capeesh?

They all nod knowing that Vince is more than capable
of dealing with any arising issues.

                    FREDDIE
               (Leaning forward)
     Yeah but…
                    VINCE
                (Cutting in)
     No yeah buts, I fucking mean it. OK?

                    FREDDIE
     *(Reluctantly, looking around at his
                    brothers)*
     Ok.

Vince see's Marcus handing a small bag of drugs over
to a man near the door, the man then hands Sammy some
cash. Vince scopes the room again and see's Charlie
Madigan with Ronnie.

                    BILLY
     (Watching Vince looking around the pub)
     So, you've seen Charlie Madigan then.

                    VINCE
                 (Bitter)
     Yeah I've seen him.

                    BILLY
             (Calming Vince down)
     Not in here Vince. Let's find out what's
     going on with Danny first.

                    VINCE
           (Looking Billy in the eye)
     When Danny wakes up, he'll put us in the
     loop. Until then, just trust me.

He gives Billy a knowing look and gets up.

                 VINCE (CONT'D)
                  (To all)
     You lot stay here. I'll be back in a minute.

Vince pours the light ale into his pint, picks it up
and audaciously heads toward Ronnie and Charlie.

CAMERA FREEZES on Ronnie and Charlie at the bar
while Vince narrates.

                    VINCE (V.O.)
Looking at the pair of them together makes
me sick. All bullshit and bravado. Looking
back, I never really trusted either of
them.

UNFREEZE. Ronnie clocks Vince and brings Charlie's
attention to him.

                    RONNIE
                 (Flash)
Hello Vince, glad you could come.

Ronnie and Vince shake hands.

                  RONNIE (CONT'D)
        (Looking in Charlie's direction)
You remember Charlie don't ya?

Vince turns to Charlie who has an UNLIT CIGAR in his
mouth.

                    VINCE
              (Shaking Charlie's hand)
Yeah, yeah course I do.

                    CHARLIE
                 (Insincerely)
Hello Vincent, good to see you again.

                    VINCE
That's Vince, only my mother called me
Vincent.

                    CHARLIE
               (Again insincerely)
Oh, sorry, it won't happen again.

Charlie forces a smile, Vince reciprocates.

                  CHARLIE (CONT'D)
Let me get you a drink, Vince.

                    VINCE
                 (Stern)
No thanks, I'm in a round with my brothers.

                    RONNIE
     I'll get the round in.

Ronnie gets the barman's attention.

                    RONNIE (CONT'D)
                 (To the barman)
     Send a couple of bottles of bubbly over to
     that table, and stick it on the slate.

Ronnie turns to Vince.

                    RONNIE (CONT'D)
                 (Sincerely)
     Call it a peace offering.

                    VINCE
                 (Sharp and abrupt)
     Oh yeah, for what exactly?

Charlie turns to talk to THREE HEAVILY BUILT MEN
standing behind him.

                    RONNIE
                 (Quietly to Vince)
     Come on Vince. Water under the bridge mate.
     We were inseparable at one time, let's let
     bygones be bygones ay, what d'ya think.

Ronnie looks sincere and offers his hand.

                    VINCE
                 (Keeping his focus)
     That's a lot of fucking water Ron.

Vince assesses the situation.

                    VINCE (CONT'D)
                 (Looking around the bar)
     For now, I'm only interested in Danny, so.

They shake hands. Ronnie tries to lighten the mood.

                    RONNIE
                 (Smiling looking at Lenny)
     Do you remember when we striped him naked
     and tied him to the lamppost outside the
     chip shop on the new estate?

They both reluctantly share a moment of reflection.

At the table, the barman brings the champagne over.
THE BARMAN IS VERY EFFEMINATE.

                    BARMAN
          (*Putting the bottle and glasses on the table*)
           The compliments of Mr Keppel.

The brother's double take as the barman is obviously
wearing MAKE-UP.

                    FREDDIE
             (*Hard, almost out of character*)
           Yeah, well we don't want it.

The barman stops and looks confused.

                    BILLY
          (*Putting his hand across Freddie's chest*)
           Shut it now little Freddie will ya.

Billy looks at the barman and smiles.

                    BILLY (CONT'D)
                (*Smiling sarcastically*)
           Sorry about my mouthy brother barman, err
           bar gender, I mean tender, that's what I
           mean, I mean bartender.

The barman sarcastically smiles back and leaves
quickly sensing some tension. The Nelson boys laugh.

                    JACK
                  (*Laughing*)
           Fucking hell Bill.

                    BILLY
     (*Starting extremely serious and finishing with a smile*)
           Let me fucking tell you something Fred.
           Never, I repeat never ever turn down free
           alcohol. That's page one on the pissheads
           guide to the gutter manual.

Jack and Freddie laugh shaking their heads.

Jack looks over at Vince laughing with Ronnie.

                    JACK
                 (Curious)
        What's Vince up too?

                    BILLY
        (Pouring himself a glass of bubbly)
        He's getting on the inside Jack, keep your
        friends close and all that shit.

Back at the bar, Charlie finishes talking with the
three men and turns to face Vince and Ronnie.

                    CHARLIE
                  (Gaudy)
        Sorry chaps, business.

Vince see's the THREE HEAVILY BUILT MEN aggressively
take two men from their table and proceed to push
them out the entrance.

                    VINCE
                  (Direct)
        What line of work are you in these days
        Charlie?
                    CHARLIE
                 (Smiling)
        Very funny Vince.

Ronnie laughs nervously.

                    VINCE
        (Not cracking a smile or taking his eyes of Charlie)
        I'm gonna join my brothers now, excuse me.

Vince walks back to the table as Ronnie and Charlie
watch on.

                    CHARLIE
        (With the smile disappearing from his face)
        Keep a close eye on him. I don't want him
        fucking things up for me.

Charlie looks right into Ronnie's eyes.

                    CHARLIE (CONT'D)
                  (Firm)
        Do I make myself clear?

                    RONNIE
                 (Shaken)
     Yeah, crystal Charlie.

Charlie moves off. A couple of friends joins Ronnie.

Vince sits down at the table with his brothers.

                    VINCE
           (Pouring himself a glass)
     I see you got the champers.

                    BILLY
                (Sarcastic)
     Yeah. Two bottles, is that it. I thought
     you had a bit of clout 'round here.

The boys laugh.

Vince notices one of THE THREE HEAVILY BUILT MEN
hand Sammy an ENVELOPE, Sammy opens it and counts
some CASH.

                    VINCE
           (Pointing at the three blokes)
     Who are the stooges?

                    JACK
                (Looking over)
     Charlie's henchmen, they reckon the black
     geezers a bit of a handful.

Vince see's Charlie looking over at him, the band
continue to play some old classics.

                    VINCE
                (Getting up)
     If I ain't back by the time this song
     finishes, come and find me.

The boys watch him get up and leave.

Vince walks toward the TOILET. He looks in the
MIRROR by the door as he enters. He sees Charlie
indicate to the THREE HEAVIES to follow him in, just
as he had anticipated.

The toilets are empty. A solitary Vince is at the URINAL but does not intend to use the toilet. We can hear the THREE HEAVILY BUILT MEN making their way in. CU of Vince clenching his fist in in anticipation.

One of the men takes up a position directly behind him, the other two either side of him.

Before a word can be said, Vince elbows the one to his right in the throat and he falls to the floor choking. He then grabs the one to his left and smashes his head into the wall. He in turn falls to the ground in a cataleptic state. The one behind him freezes in shock at how quick and efficiently Vince has dealt with his companions. Vince then pushes the palm of his hand into the bridge of the third man's nose. He also falls to the floor comatose. Vince kneels over the first thug who is disorientated and gasping for air as the other two lay motionless.

                    VINCE
          (Holding him by the throat as he chokes)
     Tell Charlie, next time he fucking tries it,
     I'm gonna kill you and more to the point,
     I'm gonna kill him. Do you understand?

The thug who is covered in blood reluctantly nods as he gasps for air. Vince throws him to the floor. Coolly Vince gets up and washes his hand in the sink before looking in the mirror.

Back at the table.

                    FREDDIE
                   (Worried)
     That's it I'm going to help him.

OTS Vince emerges from the toilet. Freddie downs his pint for Dutch courage and turns. As he does so, Vince is standing right there, nose to nose.

                    VINCE
                  (Smirking)
     Going somewhere?

                    FREDDIE
                (Slightly perturbed)
     Yeah, you lot fancy another drink?

Freddie moves to the bar slightly self-conscious,
Jack and Billy smirk as Vince sits down.

                     JACK
                 (Playfully)
        All sorted?

They all look over at the three heavies now emerging
from the toilet and making a quick exit.

                     BILLY
        It certainly looks that way to me.

Vince throws Charlie a look as Charlie watches the
three heavies scurry out the door.

Charlie slowly turns to look over at Vince. Charlie
is slightly shocked. Vince raises his glass a
reluctant Charlie reciprocates.

10   **INT. HOSPITAL – NIGHT.**   10

A Doctor enters Danny's room. George is in a camp bed
next to him. George lifts his head from the pillow as
a shaft of light from the open door hits him square
in the eyes.

                    DOCTOR
                  (Quietly)
        Mr. Nelson, can I have a quick word?

George sleepily gets up and moves toward the Doctor,
who is now outside the door.

                    GEORGE
                 (Concerned)
        Is everything ok Doc?

                    DOCTOR
            (Offering George to a chair)
        Take a seat Mr. Nelson. I've had a good look
        at the other tests and the scan we did this
        morning. The damage to his head is

significantly more serious than we had initially thought…

> GEORGE
> *(Confused)*
> What do you mean?

> DOCTOR
> *(Continuing to explain)*
> Your brother's cranium and organs have taken one hell of a beating. We are going to have to up his medication for now. Let's see if we make any advancements by the morning.

> GEORGE
> *(Panicking)*
> Shall I call my brothers?

> DOCTOR
> *(Calm)*
> No need to worry any of them just yet. Let's sees how he is in the morning. Get back into bed Mr. Nelson and get some rest, you'll be no good to anyone without getting some sleep yourself.

> GEORGE
> *(Ominously)*
> Ok Doc.

> DOCTOR
> *(Walking off)*
> Good night Mr. Nelson, try to get some rest.

> GEORGE
> *(Almost to himself)*
> Yeah, good night then.

11   **INT. THE MOON PUB/BACK ROOM – NIGHT.**   11

The boys listen to the live band.

> VINCE
> *(Standing)*
> Who wants another one?

The boys all say yes.

                          FREDDIE
                        (Standing)
          Do you want a hand?

                           VINCE
                  (Pushing him back down)
          No you're alright mate, enjoy the band.

                          FREDDIE
                   (Looking up at him)
          Alright, I'm here if you need me yeah.

Vince winks at Billy.
                           VINCE
                         (Smiling)
          I know that Fred.

As Vince moves off to the bar, he bumps into a group
of young men.

                       VINCE (CONT'D)
                        (Sincerely)
          Sorry lads.

As Vince turns back around towards the bar, he bumps
into a woman, its Lucy.

                       VINCE (CONT'D)
                         (Shocked)
          Lucy!

                           LUCY
                         (Shocked)
          Vince, what are you doing here?

                           VINCE
                (Still shocked and tongue tied)
          I, err, its, well, sorry, what was the
          question?

A broad grin appears on Vince's face.

                           LUCY
                     (Smiling coyly)
          Vince Nelson lost for words, well, that is
          a first.

They gaze at one another, still showing signs of an obvious chemistry between them.

                    VINCE
                 (Bluntly)
      Your husband invited me.

The mood sours, as they remember who and where they are.

Lucy quickly looks over at Ronnie, who is glaring right at her.

                    LUCY
                 (Sheepish)
      I'm sorry Vince I can't talk to you right
      now.

She makes to leave and he GRABS HER HAND, she turns and looks at their hands together.

CU - HANDS.

Vince lets go.

                    VINCE
                 (Infatuated)
      Sorry, I just wanted to catch up.

                    LUCY
            (Looking over at Ronnie again)
      Another time perhaps.

She moves off.

                    VINCE
               (Calling after her)
      I'll hold you to that.

Vince smiles to himself like a teenager and heads to the bar, just as Vince makes it to the bar and is about to order.
                    JACK
           (Panicking holding the phone up)
      Vince we've got to go, now.

Freddie throws Vince his coat and the boys rush out.

12   INT. HOSPITAL ENTRANCE – NIGHT.   12

As the brothers arrive, they are joined by Frank who is also rushing in. They all go through the door and head up to Danny's room. As they turn the corner, they see George slowly walking towards them in tears.

They rush to him in a panic.

> FRANK
> *(Frantic)*
> What's happened?

> GEORGE
> *(Collapsing to his knees crying)*
> He's gone. He's gone.

Frank and Jack pull George to his feet, Vince runs past him toward the room, Freddie follows.

The Doctor tries to stop Vince and talk to him, Vince brushes him aside. Vince and Freddie enter Danny's room, his corpse is covered with a bed sheet. He looks peaceful with no equipment attached to him. The lights have been dimmed.

Vince slowly pulls the sheet back to reveal Danny's dead body. Vince kisses Danny's forehead.

> VINCE
> *(Crying)*
> Why? Why you?

Billy and Frank frantically enter the room followed by Jack with his arms around George, almost holding him up. The brothers all take Danny's bedside.

THE CAMERA MOVES TO A HIGH WIDE SHOT.

CREDITS ROLL - DANNY BOY SOFTLY STARTS TO PLAY.

REFLECTION: CLOSING MONOLOGUE

I cannot begin to tell you what I felt like that day. This is not how it was supposed to end for such a young, charismatic man. Life is so precious, yet we treat it so disrespectfully. One minute you are there, the next, gone. Someone, somewhere knows what's going on and whatever happens now, I want answers, and believe me, one way or another I'm gonna get them.

FADE TO BLACK.

END OF EPISODE 2.

93

Episode 3

Answers

INTRODUCTION: OPENING MONOLOGUE

Saying goodbye to someone is never easy, especially someone so young. Over the past week or so, I've had time to think, time to cry and time to get angry. There's something I don't know, I'm not sure what, but there is something going on. It's now a case of being shrewd, I've got to make sure I get to the bottom of all this shit. In fact, I don't just want to get to the bottom of it, I'm going to get to the bottom of it. One way or another, it will be dealt with. The police are treating it as a mugging, to be fair, not that unusual for the area where they said it happened. Said that Danny fought back and in the scuffle, it went too far. Funny thing is, they never took his money, phone or in fact, they never took anything from him at all. Nah, this is no mugging, he was targeted. I wish I knew what he was up to. I can't help but think though, things could have been different if I'd of been here. I guess we'll never know.

**For every action, there is an equal and opposite reaction -
Isaac Newton**

1   **EXT. CHURCH - DAY.**   1

ESTABLISHING HIGH WIDE SHOT. It is a typical British day, FINE RAIN and overcast.

SLOW TIMESKIP OF THE FUNERAL.

We hear THE HOLLIES - 'HE AIN'T HEAVY' playing softly.

VINCE NARRATES THROUGHOUT.

The CASKET is carried out by the brothers, and lowered into the ground.

THE CAMERA SLOWLY PANS across each brother individually. We see that each one takes the loss in their own way.

A VICAR, Frank's WIFE and CHILDREN are the only other people there.

> VINCE (V.O.)
> George told everyone to let us have this moment for family only, and I'm glad people have respected that. He has suffered more than anyone has this past week or so. Like I said before he was always there for them, something I now feel I've really missed out on. I look at my brothers and how hard it has hit them too. I feel like I need to seek justice, not only for me but also for them. One thing is for sure, someone somewhere knows I'm coming, and I won't stop until I get answers.

2   **EXT/INT. THE NELSON'S/GARDEN - DAY.**   2

George stands alone in the garden, the rain falls as he looks at the masses of flowers that have been sent. Frank joins him.

> FRANK
> *(Handing George a glass of whisky)*
> Here you go mate, get that down ya.

                    GEORGE
         (Turning to see and taking the glass)
    Thanks Frank.

They both look at the flowers. Frank puts his collar
up.

                 GEORGE (CONT'D)
                    (Touched)
    It's nice so many people have sent flowers.

                     FRANK
                    (Nodding)
    Yeah. Come on mate lets go inside your
    getting soaked.

Frank puts his arm around George a guides him in.

In the lounge, Vince sits silent as does Jack
Freddie and Billy, George and Jack enter. Freddie
throws them a towel each from a pile of washing next
to him.

                 FRANK (CONT'D)
                    (Quietly)
    Thanks.

George sits. Billy pours himself a very generous
whisky.

                 FRANK (CONT'D)
              (Picking his coat up)
    I'll speak to you later George, I'm only at
    home if any of you need me.

The lads say goodbye.

                     VINCE
                   (Getting up)
    I'll walk you to your car.

They exit.

Vince and Frank walk slowly to the car.

                     FRANK
    I know you want justice Vince, but please
    be careful.

                    VINCE
Of who?

                    FRANK
Anyone. Danny's where he is for a reason
that I know.

Frank opens the car door. Vince puts his hand on it
stopping him getting in.

                    VINCE
How do you know?

                    FRANK
      (Looking to see if anyone is watching)
George would kill me if he knew I was
fuelling your fire, but your gonna do what
you do anyway so I may as well point you in
the right direction. Danny came to me about
two weeks ago…

3   **EXT. F/B FRANK'S HOUSE – NIGHT.**   3

Danny paces up and down as Frank watches.

                    DANNY
             (On edge)
Listen Frank I won't ask you again I
promise, this is the last time.

                    FRANK
             (Shaking his head)
You said that last time, and the time
before and the time before that. If I give
it to you now, you'll never learn. I'm
really sorry Dan.

                    DANNY
             (Frantic)
Please Frank, you don't understand, these
blokes are dangerous.

                    FRANK
             (Stern)
I'm sorry the answers no. If they are that
dangerous, don't get involved with them
it's as easy as that.

                    DANNY
                (*Trying everything*)
     I'll pay it back in a week I promise.
     You're my last chance Frank, Please.

                    FRANK
           (*Walking back toward the house*)
     You still owe me six hundred quid and you
     want to borrow another nine. Forget it.
     Good night Danny.

Danny looks deflated.

4   **EXT. THE NELSON'S HOUSE CONT'D – DAY.**   4

Frank and Vince continue.

                    FRANK (CONT'D)
                    (*Finishing*)
     …and that's the last time I saw him
     (pausing to look around)
     Look, speak to Freddie, he came with Danny
     a few times and asked me for money as well.
     He might know something.

Frank gets in the car, Vince leans in.

                    VINCE
                    (*Sincere*)
     Thanks Frank. That gives me something to be
     getting on with.

Vince stands upright.

                    FRANK
           (*Closing the door and opening the window*)
     Like I said before, be careful.

Vince watches Frank head off. He turns and quickly
enters the house escaping the RAIN.

5   **INT. THE MOON PUB – DAY**   5

Sammy exits the toilet wiping his nose then joins
Marcus and a group of lads.

The lads play POOL. Sammy sits with Marcus.

                    SAMMY
      (Passing Marcus a small packet under the table)
       Cheers.

                    MARCUS
           (Putting it in his pocket)
       Danny's funeral today 'aint it?

                    SAMMY
       This morning. I 'aint seen any of them for
       a few days to be fair, have you?

                    MARCUS
              (Shaking his head)
       Nah, fuck all.

Billy enters and takes a seat at the bar.

                    SAMMY
            (Pointing towards Billy)
       Fuck me talk of the devil.

                    MARCUS
               (Looking over)
       He's had a few already ain't he?

Billy looks as if he has had a skin full.

                    LENNY
         (Leaning on the bar with Billy)
       How'd it all go Bill?

                    BILLY
            (With his head in his hands)
       As well as it could Len. Load me up mate,
       whisky and plenty of it. I've got an
       appointment with a hangover and I want to
       look my best.

                    LENNY
             (Looking gutted for him)
       Sure thing Bill.
       (Looking around and filling the shot glass
       to the brim)
       This ones on me mate.

                          BILLY
              (Putting his money on the counter)
          Keep 'em coming Len, cheers.

6   **INT. THE NELSON'S LIVING ROOM - DAY.**   6

George is asleep on the sofa as Jack watches TV.
Vince sits at the dining table mulling over Frank's
words.

                          JACK
                (Looking over at Vince)
          What you up to Vince?

                          VINCE
                  (Not looking up)
          Thinking.

                          JACK
                    (Confused)
          Of what?

                          VINCE
                   (Explaining)
          My next move.

                          FREDDIE
               (Entering from the kitchen)
          I've put all the washing up away, who wants
          a cuppa?

                          JACK
          Yes please mate.

                          VINCE
                   (Looking up)
          Please.

Freddie goes back into the kitchen, Jack continues
with Vince.

                          JACK
              (Sitting at the table next to Vince)
          What we going to do then Vince?

                    VINCE
                 (Stern)
     Not sure but whatever it is, it's not gonna
     go unnoticed.

                    JACK
          (Putting his hand on Vince's shoulder)
     I'm with you all the way, count on it.

Vince looks up at him.

                    VINCE
     I might need to take you up on that.

They share a knowing look.

                    JACK
               (Face changing, sniffing)
     What the…
     (calling out)
     Freddie have you…

Freddie enters with the teas and gives Vince his
herbal tea.

                    JACK (CONT'D)
          (Face screwed up and wafting the smell)
     Fucking hell! I'm gonna watch a bit of TV
     in my room.

Jack picks his tea up and goes upstairs.

George opens his eyes and sits up.

                    GEORGE
                 (Drained)
     I'm going up to lie down.

George exits leaving Freddie and Vince alone.

                    VINCE
             (Looking to see if they are alone)
     I'm glad I've got you on your own, sit
     down.

Vince pulls a chair out next to him. Freddie sits
cautiously.

FREDDIE
(Inquisitive)
Have I done something wrong?

VINCE
(Stern but cool)
Tell me what you know about Danny and who
Danny was knocking about with.

FREDDIE
(Apprehensive)
Not much really, he done his own thing.

VINCE
Don't take me for a mug Fred, why do you
think I'm asking you? I know you know
something so let's stop the fucking
charade.

FREDDIE
(Worried)
What do you want me to say Vince? I don't
really know anything.

Freddie is uncomfortable and gets up to look out of
the window. Vince follows and looms over him
menacingly.

VINCE
(Very stern)
Look, your brother's in the cemetery, so if
you know something, tell me. Enough is
enough Fred my patience are wearing thin.

FREDDIE
(Nervous)
Why are you asking me, your making out it's
my fault?

VINCE
If you know something Freddie then tell me
'cause I'd hate to have to knock it out of
ya.

Vince spins Freddie around to face him. Freddie is
welling up almost in tears and confused at why Vince
would talk to him like that.

                    VINCE
                 (Unfazed)
      Don't cry for fuck sake.

A tear runs down Freddie's face.

                   FREDDIE
           (Crying raising his voice)
      Why are you picking on me? I'm your brother
      too you know.

                    VINCE
      I'm here to sort this shit out and I know
      you know something.

                   FREDDIE
      He knocked around with loads of people,
      what can I say.

Vince walks around him.

                    VINCE
      You're a fucking liar Freddie. You went to
      Frank and asked to borrow money, what was
      that for?

                   FREDDIE
              (Shocked that he knows)
      It was for Danny alright.

Freddie tries to walk away and Vince stops him.

                    VINCE
                (Raised voice)
      Drugs maybe, is that it?

                   FREDDIE
                  (Stunned)
      What?

                    VINCE
      Off who? Just give me a name.

Freddie tries to walk away as Vince pushes him into
the armchair.

Vince walks over to him and grabs his collar.

                    GEORGE (O.C.)
          Let him go.

Vince and Freddie look over to the doorway. George
is standing there. Vince lets Freddie go.
Vince stands upright and faces George, Freddie gets
up and straightens himself out then heads to the
door.

                      FREDDIE
                    (Shocked)
          Fuck this I'm going to see Billy.

Freddie exits, George and Vince stare at each other.
George Walks over to the window and looks as Freddie
walk down the street.

                      GEORGE
          What do you think you're playing at?

                      VINCE
                (Slightly embarrassed)
          I wanna find out what happened to Danny
          that's all. I weren't gonna hit him.

                      GEORGE
                    (Hard)
          Who the fuck do you think you are? You come
          here after all this time then swagger
          around like you own the place. You're
          pushing your own brother around like you're
          a fucking terrorist interrogator. If he
          said he don't know anything, then he don't.
          Take his fucking word for it.

                      VINCE
                    (Sure)
          I know that…

                      GEORGE
                (Firm, cutting in)
          With all due respect Vince, you know fuck
          all. You don't know little Freddie from a
          pot of jam. If you want to bully anyone
          then bully me.

George fronts Vince and pushes him.

GEORGE (CONT'D)
Well come on big man, have a pop at me.

VINCE
(Moving away)
Leave it out George, all I was trying to do
was find out a little bit about Danny…

GEORGE
(Snapping)
Did you try asking him?

Vince just looks at George knowing he could be
right.

GEORGE (CONT'D)
(Calming)
I thought not. Danny's gone Vince and I
know you're beating yourself up because you
never got a chance to know him properly,
but it's not our fault.

VINCE
(Calm)
Look Frank told me about Danny and Freddie
asking him to borrow money. I'm thinking
for drugs.

GEORGE
I think your right. Danny got himself
involved with some shady people but not
Freddie, that I can assure you.

VINCE
So why would Freddie want that sort of cash
then?

GEORGE
(Sitting down)
Frank never asks the reasons when any of us
wants to borrow money. He either lends it
or he don't. Freddie has been saving up for
about a year or so now.

VINCE
(Intrigued)
For what?

                    GEORGE
To come and see you Vince. You're his idol,
the boy don't stop talking about you. The
fact that your just like Dad, your
reputation, your character, everything.
That's why what you have just done must
have hurt him more than you could ever
know.

                    VINCE
              (Head in hands)
Fuck! What am I doing?

                    GEORGE
       (Putting his hand on Vince's shoulder)
Go and talk to him. He is a great kid once
you get to know him.

Vince looks at George knowing he is right.

7   **INT. THE MOON PUB – DAY.**   7

Billy sits at the bar, now really drunk. Sammy and
Marcus sit down either side of him. Billy is slumped
on the bar stool with his eyes barely open, as a
concerned Lenny looks on. Marcus has a shot glass,
he is trying to place it into billy's hand.

                    MARCUS
          (Patronising and laughing)
Here you go Billy mate I've got you another
one.

Billy just about lifts his head up and downs the
drink spilling most of it down his face and shirt.
The two of them laugh.

                    SAMMY
                 (Giggling)
Lenny pour another.

                    LENNY
                (Concerned)
I don't think he needs…

                    SAMMY
          (Stern, through gritted teeth)
Pour him another one you mug.

Lenny does exactly as he is told, then hands the
shot glass over.

Freddie enters in the background. Lenny goes over to
him.

                    FREDDIE
              (Looking over at Billy)
        What the fuck's going on over there?

                     LENNY
                   (Worried)
        Oh Fred, they're taking the piss out of
        him.

Freddie walks around the bar and knocks the drink
out of a semi-conscious Billy's hand.

                    FREDDIE
                   (Stern)
        That's enough. Have some respect.

Sammy and Marcus reluctantly make room for Freddie
to take Billy's side.

                     SAMMY
                   (Narked)
        Who the fuck do you think you're talking
        to?

                    FREDDIE
                  (Unnerved)
        He's done nothing wrong to you, leave him
        alone.

Freddie helps Billy sit upright.

                     SAMMY
               (In Freddie's face)
        Mouthy little fucker 'aint ya? You'd best
        say sorry. Now.

Lenny looks uneasy.

                     LENNY
             (Trying to calm things down)
        Come on lads let's not…

                    MARCUS
                 (To Lenny)
      Shut yer-fucking mouth Len.

Lenny backs off.

                    SAMMY
               (Poking Freddie)
      You heard me. Say sorry.

                    FREDDIE
      *(Swallowing hard, looking around at
                Sammy's mates)*
      Sorry alright. Look we don't want any
      trouble ok.

                    SAMMY
                 (Smarmy)
      Now that's what I call respect. If you ever
      talk to me like that again I'll open you
      up, do you understand?

                    FREDDIE
             (Looking sheepish)
      We just don't want any trouble Sammy,
      that's all.

Freddie helps Billy off his stool and tries to take
him towards to door.

                    BILLY
                 (Mumbling)
      Where are we going Fleddie?

                    FREDDIE
             (Quietly to Billy)
      I'm taking you home mate.

As Freddie and Billy's backs are turned, Marcus
punches Freddie in the ribs. Freddie and Billy
collapse and Marcus grabs Freddie around the throat.

                    MARCUS
                  (Firm)
      You listen to me you little wanker, tell
      your brother Vince if he wants some he
      knows where I am.

CU on Freddie we see his EYES FLICK TO THE LEFT and back again.

                    FREDDIE
          (Pulling Marcus's hand away)
      Tell him yourself.

Marcus stands up looking confused and turns around. As he does, we reveal Vince standing behind him.

Before a word can be said, Vince punches Marcus on the chin and he drops like a sack of potatoes.

                    VINCE
            (Looking at Freddie)
    Pick Billy up and let's go home.

Vince turns to a stunned Sammy as Freddie gets billy to his feet.

Vince walks around an unconscious Marcus towards Sammy as Sammy slowly backs away.

8   **INT. RONNIE'S OFFICE, RED LION – DAY.**   8

We see Ronnie sitting at his desk with a cigar in one hand and a whisky in the other. He has clearly been watching this exchange on his hi-tech CC TV MONITOR. He zooms in on Vince.

Vince walks toward Sammy cont'd.

Intercut with scene 7.

                    VINCE
             (Pointing)
    I don't give a fuck who you think you are
    son or who you think your old man is. If
    you ever fuck about with my family again I
    will be back for you, do you understand?

Vince doesn't wait for an answer. Ronnie zooms out as the Nelson boys leave.

Still watching the monitor, we see him dial a number on the PHONE the display reeds CHARLIE MOBILE, the phone starts to ring.

                    CHARLIE (O.C.)
          Hello Ronnie, what's up?

Ronnie sips his whisky and zooms in on Sammy and
Lenny picking Marcus up from the floor.

                    RONNIE
          We need to talk about Vince
          Nelson.

9   **INT. THE NELSON'S HOUSE – DAY.**   9

Freddie walks down the stairs and into the kitchen
as Vince is pouring himself and Freddie a cup of
tea.

                    FREDDIE
               (Trying not to look Vince in the eye)
          Well that's Billy down for the night.

Vince smiles and hands Freddie a cup of tea.

                    VINCE
          Here you go mate. I think you deserve it.

                    FREDDIE
               (Taking the tea)
          Thanks Vince.
          (He slowly sips it)
          Did George leave a note?

Passing Freddie a note, Freddie opens it.

                    VINCE
               (Sheepish)
          He's gone shopping. Look, I'm sorry
          alright, genuinely, I'm really sorry.

                    FREDDIE
               (Chuffed)
          It's ok. I know everyone is up in the
          air at the moment. No harm done.

                    VINCE
               (Impressed)
          That was a brave thing you did for your
          brother today.

                    FREDDIE
                  (Chuffed)
Nah, it was nothing. I would of done it for
any of you lot.

                    VINCE
I know would, but sometimes you have to
think. You could have got yourself into a
lot of trouble.

                    FREDDIE
I could have handled it.

Vince looks at Freddie reassuringly and winks.

                 FREDDIE (CONT'D)
          (A big smile comes across his face)
Did you see the way he went down (mocking
the punch)
Crack and that was that. Goodnight Vienna.

                    VINCE
                  (Smiling)
Yeah, I think he got the message.

Freddie laughs.

                 VINCE (CONT'D)
Tell me Fred, was Danny mixed up with Sammy
somehow?

Looking at Vince in a different light.

                    FREDDIE
                 (Ready to talk)
I saw him once or twice with him in the
pub. Danny had his mates and I've got mine,
but we always looked out for one another.

                    VINCE
Did you ever see anything out of the
ordinary?

                    FREDDIE
                 (Remembering)
There was this one night I woke up and
heard voices outside…

10   EXT. F/B THE NELSON'S HOUSE – NIGHT.   10

                    FREDDIE (CONT'D, V.O.)
          Danny was standing by this Merc with
          Marcus. They were talking to someone in the
          car but I couldn't really see who. I would
          assume Sammy, but I can't be sure. I could
          hear raised voices, so I called out the
          window to see if he was ok.

Freddie from the window.

                         FREDDIE
                    (Trying to get a better look)
          Dan, you alright mate?

Danny and Marcus look up to the window.

                          DANNY
                      (Calling up)
          Yeah fine, go back to bed.

Danny then turns back to Marcus.

                          DANNY
                      (Explaining)
          Little Freddie, bless him.

                         MARCUS
                        (Stern)
          This is it Danny, you won't get a second
          chance.

11   INT. THE NELSON'S HOUSE CONT'D – DAY.   11

Vince and Freddie at the table.

                      FREDDIE (CONT'D)
                    (Sipping his tea)
          …and that was about it.

                          VINCE
                (Putting his hand on Freddie's)
          Thank you Fred, that's all I needed mate.

Vince gets up and puts his coat on. Freddie looks up
at him.

                    FREDDIE
         Where are you going?

                    VINCE
         I'm going to have a chat with someone.

                    FREDDIE
                 (Getting up)
         I'm coming with you.

                    VINCE
                 (Thinking quick)
         You can't. Someone has to stay here and
         look after Billy.

Freddie nods.

                    FREDDIE
                 (Feeling part of things)
         Ok I'll do that, and I'll see you when you
         get back, yeah?

                    VINCE
                 (Winking)
         That's it mate, see ya later.

Freddie watches Vince leave, but has a worried look
in his eyes.

12   **INT. INDIAN RESTAURANT – DAY.**   12

Charlie sits at a table in a HIGH-CLASS INDIAN
RESTAURANT, with a WINE BOTTLE in a COOLER and a
half full glass. Ronnie enters and heads over to the
table. Charlie is eating POPPADUM'S and reading THE
TIMES.

                    CHARLIE
                 (Still reading and not looking up)
         Take a seat. Help yourself to a glass.

A waiter comes over and pours Ronnie a drink, Ronnie
looks slightly nervous.

                    CHARLIE
                 (Folding his paper up and looking at Ronnie)
         What's the problem now?

                         RONNIE
        Vince knocked Marcus out in the pub today.

                         CHARLIE
                    (Tucking into his grub)
        Well he clearly ain't lost his touch then
        has he.

                         RONNIE
        I think he knows Danny was involved in
        something.

                         CHARLIE
                        (Smug)
        His brother was mugged, end of.

Charlie loads his plate up.

                         RONNIE
                       (Unsure)
        Do you really think he's gonna let it be
        now Danny's dead.

                         CHARLIE
                   (Looking at Ronnie)
        Relax, Patterson's on the case. It's
        sorted, boy comes home from the pub, boy
        gets mugged, boy dies. Shit happens.

Ronnie still looks worried.

                         CHARLIE
                       (Unfazed)
        Want a poppadum?

Charlie looks nonchalant.

13   **EXT. THE MOON PUB - DAY.**   13

        Vince walks toward the pub, a car door opens and
        Delgado steps out in front of him blocking his path.

        Vince is slightly taken back but ready for trouble.

        Vince sees another man step out of the passenger
        side into the shadows, he cannot get a good look at
        his face until the man walks around the car in front

of Vince. It's Patterson. If looks could kill, Vince
contains his anger.

                    PATTERSON
                  (Sarcastic)
     Well Well Well, the prodigal son returns.
     Long-time Vincent.

Patterson looks him up and down.

                     VINCE
               (Holding back his anger)
     You saw to that didn't ya? What do you
     want?

                    PATTERSON
                  (Smirking)
     That's nice after all this time Vincent. So
     where are you off to on this fine night
     then?

Vince looks over to THE MOON PUB.

                     VINCE
                  (Sarcastic)
     Where do you think? I'll leave that for you
     and Makepeace to work out.

Vince walks around the two men. Patterson calls out
after him.

                    PATTERSON
                  (Calling out)
     I'll be watching you Vincent.

Vince stops but does not turn back.

                 PATTERSON (CONT'D)
                (Coolly smiling)
     Bet your life I'll be watching you. So
     let's not start being a silly boy, because
     I know a nice little bed and breakfast on
     the Isle of Wight that would accommodate a
     scumbag like you.

                     VINCE
     No problem. Oh and its Vince by the way.

Vince holds his middle finger up to them over his shoulder as he continues on his journey.

                    DELGADO
               (Concerned)
That was a bit harsh Guv.

                    PATTERSON
          (Turning his attention to Delgado)
That sort of man deserves no mercy. You'll understand that one day Delgado.

Patterson patronisingly pats Delgado's shoulder and moves to get into the car.

14   INT. THE MOON PUB – DAY.   14

Vince enters the pub and heads over to Lenny.

                    VINCE
          (Getting Lenny's attention, quietly)
Len, has Ronnie been in?

                    LENNY
          (Turning to face Vince)
He was here when you sparked Marcus.

                    VINCE
               (Frowning)
Where?

                    LENNY
               (Pointing)
In his office. He left shortly after you and he looked pissed right off.

                    VINCE
               (Quizzical)
Did he say where he was going?

                    LENNY
Do me a favor Vince, he don't even look at me let alone tell me what he's up to.

                    VINCE
Danny got himself mixed up with some dodgy people. I think he was selling drugs for someone. What do you know about it?

                    LENNY
                  (Sincere)
     If I knew anything, I would tell you.

Lenny looks around to make sure their conversation
is private.

                 LENNY (CONT'D)
                   (Quiet)
     Try the snooker hall. I overhear some of
     the lads talking about someone called Fat
     Tony. It might be something, it might be
     nothing, but that is all I can think of.

Vince stands.

                    VINCE
                  (Grateful)
     Thanks Len, if you hear anything bell Jack
     and he'll get hold of me.

Vince walks toward the door.

                    LENNY
     See ya soon Vince.

Vince turns and nods in appreciation.

15   **INT/EXT. SNOOKER HALL – DAY.**   15

Vince walks into the SNOOKER HALL and over to the
BARMAN.

The hall is long and narrow with around 12 POOL
TABLES leading to the back of the hall where SIX
LADS are playing a game of killer. They are drinking
and laughing aloud.

                    BARMAN
               (Smiling at Vince)
     Hello mate can I help you?

                    VINCE
                (Smiling back)
     I hope so mate. I'm looking for Tony.

                    BARMAN
              (Frowning with curiosity)
     Tony who?

                    VINCE
               (Playing the game)
     Fat Tony.

                    BARMAN
                (Still cautious)
     He's not here. Who wants to know anyway?

                    VINCE
          (Looking at the barman stern)
     (Pause) Me.

Vince slowly takes in the surroundings and sees the
lads at the end of the hall.

                 VINCE (CONT'D)
                   (Coolly)
     Mind if I ask around?

Vince points to the lads.

                    BARMAN
               (With a wry smile)
     Whatever mate, be my guest.

                    VINCE
               (Sarcastically)
     Thank you.

Vince turns and slowly walks toward the lads. The
barman grins thinking Vince will soon be put in his
place.

As Vince nears the lads, they notice him. A BIG LAD
named KELVIN, who obviously works out stands to
greet him.

                    KELVIN
              (Poking his chest out)
     Yeah?
                    VINCE
          (Looking him up and down, cool)
     Any of you know where I can find fat Tony?

                    KELVIN
                   (Stern)
     Who wants him?

                    VINCE
          (Getting tired of the games)
     I do.

                    KELVIN
            (Walking toward Vince)
       I'll tell you…

Before he finishes his sentence, Vince knocks him
out, lightning quick. Kelvin slumps to the floor,
the lads are startled.

                    VINCE
                  (Sighing)
       Lads I'm not the patient sort, so let's
       stop fucking about shall we?

Vince turns to one of the lads.

                    VINCE (CONT'D)
                  (Focused)
       Fat Tony, where is he?

                    LAD 2
                  (Nervous)
       He'll be here later.

Vince leans in as the lad nervously backs
against the wall.

                    VINCE
                  (Smirking)
       Thank you.

Vince turns and walks down the snooker hall. One of
the lads picks his phone up and DIALS A NUMBER.

SPLIT SCREEN - as the lad watches Vince walk toward
the exit.

                    LAD 3
                (On the phone)
       Tone, some nutter has just knocked Kelvin
       spark out and he's looking for you.

SPLIT SCREEN.

                    FAT TONY
          (Getting out of his motor, eating crisps)
     Where are you?

                    LAD 3
          (Watching Vince leave the building)
     At the snooker hall.

                    FAT TONY
          (Pressing the key fob to lock his car)
     I've just got here.

As he turns, we go FULL SCREEN as he is punched
in the face.

Vince then pins a stunned tony on the bonnet of his
car. Tony NOSE IS BLEEDING. He squirms uncomfortably
almost in the foetal position.

                    FAT TONY (CONT'D)
               (Scared)
     Pease don't hit me again.

Fat Tony is close to tears.

                    VINCE
               (Firm)
     I'm Vince Nelson, Danny's brother.

Vince lets Tony up. Tony straightens himself out and
stands nervously in front of Vince.

                    VINCE (CONT'D)
               (Firm)
     I need answers.

                    FAT TONY
          (Looking around the car park)
     Not here man.
     (Tony opens the car with the fob)
     Get in.

Vince cautiously gets in, as does Tony.

16   INT. LENNY'S BEDSIT – DAY.   16

Lenny sits in a SMALL CLUTTERED BEDSIT in an armchair, with the phone on a small table in front of him. He picks up the phone and pulls out a small crumpled up piece of paper from his pocket. He starts to cry as he dials the number.

LENNY
(Looking distressed)

Hello *(pause)* yeah it's me, I'm ready to talk *(pause)* I'm at home *(pause)* ok, see you then.

Lenny sobs as he puts the phone down.

17   INT. KEPPEL'S HOME – DAY.   17

Lucy answers the front door. It is Charlie with some flowers.

CHARLIE
(Leaning in to kiss Lucy)

Hello sweetheart.

He gives her the flowers and enters.

LUCY
(Surprised)

Hello Dad, this is a nice surprise. What brings you here?

CHARLIE
(Smiling)

I was passing and thought I'd pop in. Put the kettle on dear.

Charlie sits in the armchair and makes himself at home.

LUCY
(Calling out from the kitchen)

Would you like coffee, I've just made some?

CHARLIE
(Calling back)

Yes please love.

Charlie slowly looks around then picks up a picture
from the side table next to his chair. Its Lucy,
Ronnie and Sammy.

Lucy enters with two cups. Charlie puts the picture
down and takes the cup.

                    CHARLIE
                (Smiling)
        Cheers love.

Lucy sits on the sofa and turns the TV off by the
remote ready to chat.

                    LUCY
            (Putting her coffee down)
        So, how have you been? You're looking very
        well.

                    CHARLIE
            (Putting his coffee down)
        Thanks darling, I've been fine. I've just
        brought a place in Nice, its right on the
        sea front. It's beautiful.

                    LUCY
                (Interested)
        Has Mum seen it?

                    CHARLIE
        Not yet. She's going on Monday in fact,
        that's sort of why I'm here. I was
        wondering if you wanted to go with her,
        take Sammy, and make a thing of it.

                    LUCY
                (Surprised)
        Well it's a bit sudden Dad. I will have to
        talk to Ronnie first and see what he's got
        on.

                    CHARLIE
            (Picking up his coffee)
        Ronnie and I have some business to take
        care of. I was thinking just you Sammy and
        your Mum, you know a bit of time for
        relaxing.

                    LUCY
                 (*Curiously*)
This business, is it anything to do with
Vince Nelson?

                  CHARLIE
                 (*Coolly*)
Why would it be anything to do with him?

                    LUCY
                (*Cautiously*)
Well I thought what with his brother Danny
and all…

                  CHARLIE
                (*Cutting in*)
That's none of our business. We are well
shot of that scumbag. (Inquisitive)
Ain't we?

                    LUCY
                (*Stumbling*)
Yeah. Yeah of course we are.

                  CHARLIE
                (*Softening*)
He was all wrong for you and you knew it.

                    LUCY
            (*Holding back, covering*)
Come on Dad, that was twenty years ago,
what do you think I am. He turned out to be
a wrong 'en anyway.

                  CHARLIE
         (*Changing the subject and standing*)
Well that settles it. I'll tell your Mother
you're going with her.

Charlie walks toward the door. He kisses Lucy.

                    LUCY
             (*Seeing her father off*)
I'll call Mum in a while.

> CHARLIE
> *(Leaving)*
Love you sweetheart.

Lucy closing the door.

> LUCY
> *(Smiling)*
Ok, love you Dad.

She closes the door and stands against it pondering. She knows something is not as it seems.

18   **INT/EXT. BRICK YARD – DAY.**   18

Tony pulls up between some derelict houses and then turns the ignition off. He has some rolled up tissue in his nose to stop the bleeding.

> FAT TONY
> *(Looking around)*
No one ever comes down here, we're safe to talk.

Fat Tony turns to Vince.

> VINCE
> *(Unsure of why Tony has brought him to this place)*
What's going on? It's like you were expecting a visit.

> FAT TONY
> *(Pulling a joint from his pocket)*
It helps me relax.

He moves to light it.

> FAT TONY (CONT'D)
> *(Nervous)*
You don't mind do you?

Vince takes the joint out of Tony's mouth and discards it.

> VINCE
> *(Stern)*

Yeah. I do as it happens, how did you know
I was coming?

> FAT TONY
> *(Looking at Vince)*

I knew someone was coming, weren't sure who
would be first.

> VINCE
> *(Intrigued)*

What do you mean?

> FAT TONY
> *(Explaining)*

The moneymen, the muscle, the old bill, any
of them.

> VINCE
> *(Taking an interest)*

I think you'd better start talking.

Fat Tony nods then gets himself comfortable.

> FAT TONY
> *(Explaining)*

All the gear from the estate is knocked out
through me. They supply the gear and I
supply the junkies, everyone is a winner.

Tony looks at Vince who is expressionless, gathers
himself and carries on.

19   **INT. F/B SNOOKER HALL – NIGHT.**   19

The snooker hall is empty, Fat Tony and Marcus stand
at the snooker table counting out THOUSANDS OF
POUNDS.

> MARCUS
> *(Counting the money)*

It's still nine hundred short.

> FAT TONY
> *(Friendly)*

Fuck sake, nine hundred. I've given you
just over eleven grand.

                              MARCUS
                    (*Pulling his phone out and dialling*)
              Yeah but the boss wants twelve.

                             FAT TONY
                             (*Hassled*)
              I'll get it in the week…

Marcus holds his finger up on Tony's lips to silence
him, and then talks into the phone.

                              MARCUS
                        (*Into the phone*)
              You'd better come in.

Marcus hangs up.

20   **INT/EXT. BRICK YARD CONT'D – DAY.**   20

Tony in mid-explanation.

                              VINCE
                            (*Guessing*)
           Sammy?

                             FAT TONY
                        (*Shaking his head*)
           No.

21   **INT. F/B SNOOKER HALL CONT'D – NIGHT**   21

The door to the snooker hall opens, Fat Tony and
Marcus watch as the two figures walk forward to
reveal PATTERSON AND RONNIE.

                            PATTERSON
                      (*As they near the table*)
           Anthony, who could it be this time.

                             FAT TONY
                             (*Scared*)
           Give me a couple of days, please.

                              RONNIE
                              (*Hard*)
           We set you up in this place for a reason
           Tone, you sort our shit out and we look
           after you.

                    PATTERSON
                  (Cutting in)
The problem is you keep fucking things up,
don't ya?

Ronnie walks behind Tony.

                    FAT TONY
I'll have the money in the morning.

                    RONNIE
              (Into his ear quietly)
Not good enough I'm afraid. Me and Mr
Patterson are going to leave now and you
are gonna tell Marcus the name of the
arsehole that keeps paying up late.

                    PATTERSON
               (Leaning into Tony)
The arsehole that is taking us for mugs.

Patterson and Ronnie slowly walk away.

22   INT/EXT. BRICK YARD CONT'D - DAY   22

Vince listens carefully to Tony.

                 FAT TONY (CONT'D)
                    (Upset)
Danny was my mate Vince. I tried to cover
him the best I could.

                     VINCE
                   (Softening)
So, Patterson and Ronnie run all the drugs
on the estate?

                    FAT TONY
They work for Sammy's granddad...

                     VINCE
Charlie Madigan.

                    FAT TONY
Yeah, Charlie Madigan. He's a dangerous
man. He runs everything and everyone, he's
very well connected.

                    VINCE
So you own the snooker hall then?

                    FAT TONY
               (Shaking his head)
Nah. My name is on all the paper work, but
Charlie owns it. Charlie owns everything.

                    VINCE
                  (Curious)
Why are you telling me all this?

                    FAT TONY
              (Confessing, softly)
Conscience I suppose. Danny was my mate and
they took the fucking piss with him.
Whoever done that to him needs sorting out
and the word is you're the man.

                    VINCE
                  (Focused)
Where will I find Marcus on his own?

                    FAT TONY
He lives down near Fieldway shops in the
flats. I'll drop you off around the corner.

They exchange a look. Vince offers tony his hand.

                    VINCE
Thank you. Sorry about your nose. Good job
I didn't hit you too hard.

                    FAT TONY
What? Listen, good luck alright. Just be
careful.

Tony starts the car and they pull off.

CREDITS ROLL.

REFLECTION: CLOSING MONOLOGUE

People are starting to see how far I am willing to go. It's
not going to be pretty by a long chalk, but it is gonna be
finished. I'm getting closer and closer to the answers I need,
but I've got a feeling that there is much more to this story
than I've found out so far. One thing is for sure, whatever
the process, the outcome will definitely be the same. Time
will tell.

FADE TO BLACK.

END OF EPISODE 3.

133

Episode 4

An eye for an eye

INTRODUCTION: OPENING MONOLOGUE

Whatever I do now is definitely not going to go unnoticed. All I have to do is try and keep my brothers out of it. Things are starting to come together. I have to keep my nose clean long enough to get justice for Danny.

Courage is knowing what not to fear – Plato

1   INT. VINCE'S BEDROOM – MORNING.   1

Freddie, with a cup of tea opens Vince's bedroom
door and wakes him. Vince looks over at Jack's empty
bed.

                         VINCE
              (Rubbing his eyes and yawning)
        Where's Jack?

                         FREDDIE
                 (Handing Vince his tea)
        He's downstairs.

                         VINCE
                    (Sitting up)
        Tell everyone we need a chat, ring Frank
        and wake Billy up. Downstairs in half hour,
        ok?

                         FREDDIE
                     (Curious)
        Are we getting things done today?

                         VINCE
        Yeah, we're getting things done. Downstairs
        in half hour.
        (Vince winks at Freddie)
        Sort it for me, ok mate?

                         FREDDIE
                     (Proudly)
        I'm on it.

Freddie leaves the room. Vince gets up and walks to
the FULL-LENGTH MIRROR in his underwear. We can hear
Freddie organising downstairs.

                    GRACE NELSON (O.C.)
        Don't go getting yourself into any more
        trouble Vincent.

CONFUSED, VINCE TURNS TO LOOK.

CU VINCE

THE CAMERA 360'S AROUND VINCE TO REVEAL.

F/B

Vince stands facing a BEAUTIFULLY PRESENTED WOMAN.

                    VINCE
                 (Stunned)
      Mum.

Vince picks a towel up from the back of the
chair to cover his dignity.

                    GRACE NELSON
                 (Smiling)
      Oh, do me a favour Vince. I've seen it all
      before.

Grace walks over to the window and OPENS THE
CURTAINS.

                    GRACE NELSON
      It's a beautiful day out Vince, it'd be a
      shame to spoil it.

She turns to face Vince.

                    GRACE NELSON
                 (Looking at a stunned Vince sternly)
      Make sure you know what you're doing,
      because things could get very messy.

Vince is welling up.

                    VINCE
                 (Unable to speak)
      I've got to…

The bedroom door opens. Vince turns to see Freddie.

WHIP PAN - PRESENT DAY.

                    FREDDIE
                 (Peeking around the door)
      Jack's made bacon sarnies.

                    VINCE
                 (Confused)
      Yeah cheers, I'll be down in a sec.

Freddie leaves Vince looks around the room then slowly walks over and OPENS THE CURTAINS.

2   INT. POLICE STATION – INT.   2

Delgado sits at his desk, busy on the computer as Patterson walks in.

                    PATTERSON
          (Entering the room and hanging his jacket
                        up)
Good morning.

                    DELGADO
             (Looking up)
Morning Guv.

                    PATTERSON
          (Looking through some mail)
What we got today then.

                    DELGADO
          (Still on the computer)
Not much for us. Do you know anyone called Anthony Ahmet?

                    PATTERSON
          (Not really interested)
No, don't ring a bell. Why?

                    DELGADO
          (Looking at a slip of paper)
We had an anonymous call late last night. Apparently, he deals a bit of coke according to this. Quite a bit.

                    PATTERSON
          (Looking up, interested)
What was his name again?

                    DELGADO
          (Looking at the paper)
Err. Anthony Ahmet. He goes by the name of Fat Tony. Don't he own the snooker club?

Standing to lean over the desk.

                    PATTERSON
                    (*Quick*)
        Give me that, I'll look into that today.

Patterson takes the piece of paper and walks to the
other side of the room where the COFFEE MACHINE is
and selects a coffee.

Patterson opens his phone and dials a number.

                    PATTERSON
        We'll drop by and see what the Nelson boys
        are up to as well.

The phone is answered, it's Marcus.

SPLIT SCREEN.

                    MARCUS
                    (*In bed*)
        Hello.

                    PATTERSON
                    (*Quietly*)
        Get your arse around to Fat Tony and get
        all the money he owes.

                    MARCUS
                    (*Waking up*)
        Yeah, is there a problem?

Patterson hangs up. FULL SCREEN.

Delgado watches curiously from over Patterson's
shoulder.

3   **INT. THE NELSON'S DINING ROOM - DAY.**   3

Vince stands at the end of the table that George,
Billy and Jack are sitting at. Freddie is perched on
the end of the sofa. Frank enters. The brother looks
over to him.

                    FRANK
                    (*Coming in the door*)
        I got here as quick as I could.

                    GEORGE
              (Offering Frank a seat)
It's ok mate. sit down.

FRANK SITS.

                    VINCE
              (Leaning on the table)
I found out a few things last night.

                    JACK

Like what?

                    VINCE

Danny got himself mixed up with some bad
characters. He was knocking out cocaine.

Vince turns to Freddie.

                    VINCE (CONT'D)
What can you tell us Fred?

                    FREDDIE
              (Shaking his head)
As I said before, he done his own thing. I
don't know nothing.

                    VINCE
              (Turning to Jack)
What can you tell me about Marcus?

                    JACK
              (Leaning back)
Nothing really. He's from out of town.
Bermondsey I think, other than that
nothing.

                    GEORGE
              (To Billy)
What have you heard in the pub?

                    BILLY
Not much other than when Ronnie or Charlie
are about everyone seems to bend over
backwards for them. Lenny might be able to
shed some light on something, he looks like
he's on the verge of a breakdown though. He
might be ready to talk.

                    GEORGE
                (At his wits end)
        What do you want to do Vince?

The boys all look to Vince for guidance.

                    VINCE
                 (With a plan)
        Frank, Jack, you two go back to work.
        Freddie, get yourself ready and help George
        get some food in.
        (Vince hands George two £50 notes) Bill go
        and see what you can find out at the
        boozer.

Billy stands and puts his coat on.

                    BILLY
        I'm on it.

                    VINCE
        I'm gonna have a quiet word with Marcus.

                    GEORGE
                 (Cautious)
        We all want Justice Vince, but please don't
        let this get out of hand.

Vince opens the door ready to leave.

                    VINCE
                (Turning back)
        It's already out of hand George.

Vince leaves and the brothers look at one another.

4   **INT/EXT. KEPPEL'S HOUSE – DAY.**   **4**

Lucy is putting some bits in the sink as Ronnie
enters and kisses her on the cheek.

                    RONNIE
            (Rushing to put his jacket on)
        Good morning babe.

                    LUCY
    (With her back to him, going through the motions)
        Good morning.

She turns to face him and smiles.

> RONNIE
> *(Drinking some juice and picking up his keys)*
> Is Sammy up yet?

> LUCY
> *(Handing him his briefcase)*
> He's in the shower.

> RONNIE
> *(Uninterested)*
> I'll be home around four, see you later.

Ronnie leaves not even waiting for a reply.

> LUCY
> *(Almost to herself)*
> Yeah, goodbye.

Sammy enters and kisses her on the cheek as he makes to leave.

> SAMMY
> *(Rushing)*
> Who you talking to?

Sammy opens the door.

> SAMMY (CONT'D)
> *(Closing the door)*
> Bye Mum.

> LUCY
> *(Dejected)*
> No one, as usual.

5   **EXT/INT. MARCUS'S FLAT – DAY.**   5

A YOUNG ATTRACTIVE LADY exits the flat.

> VINCE
> *(Running toward the door)*
> Hold the door please.

                    YOUNG LADY
                     (Smiling)
     There you go.

                      VINCE
                     (Smiling)
     Thanks.

Vince takes the door and holds it open for the lady.
She looks Vince up and down.

                   VINCE (CONT'D)
                     (Coolly)
     You don't happen to know which flat Marcus
     lives in do you?

                    YOUNG LADY
     Not sure, sorry.

                      VINCE
                    (Explaining)
     He's about six foot, moody looking.

                    YOUNG LADY
                    (Thinking)
     Mixed race?

                      VINCE
                     (Smiling)
     Yeah that's him.

                    YOUNG LADY
     Top floor. Flat six.

                      VINCE
     Thank you, you're a star.

                    YOUNG LADY
                     (Coyly)
     You're welcome.

Vince sees her leave then takes to the stairs. As he
reaches flat six the door opens to reveal Marcus.

Marcus sees Vince, and then tries to shut the door.
Vince pushes Marcus into the flat and onto the
floor.

                    VINCE
              (Holding Marcus down)
I want to talk to you.

                    MARCUS
                (Petrified)
Fuck this. Look mate this is bigger than
me. I don't want any part of it.

                    VINCE
I'm gonna let you up now. Don't do anything
silly or it gonna really hurt, do you
understand?

                    MARCUS
               (Sarcastically)
Mate, I've never been hit that hard in all
my life.

Vince rags him.

                    VINCE
             (Through gritted teeth)
Do you understand?

                    MARCUS
                (In quickly)
I understand, I understand.

Vince slowly lets Marcus up. They move cautiously
into the front room. The contents of the flat have
been packed up into boxes, ready for moving.

                    VINCE
           (Curiously looking around)
Going somewhere?

Vince looks around as Marcus sits on the edge of the
sofa.

                    MARCUS
            (Straightening himself out)
This is all too much for me. I've had
enough.

                    VINCE
Do you know why I'm here?

                    MARCUS
                (Nodding gingerly)
    Yeah, I'll tell you now it was nothing to
    do with me. I never touched him that night.

                    VINCE
                (Calm)
You were there?

                    MARCUS
        (Ashamed, holding his head in his hands)
    Yeah. I was there.

                    VINCE
                (Calm)
    I wanna know every detail.

Marcus nods.

6   **EXT. F/B STREETS - NIGHT.**   6

We see a cold wet street. Danny stands alone by the
closed KEBAB SHOP. The street is desolate. Danny
looks nervously at his watch.

                MARCUS (V.O.)
    We were looking for him everywhere that
    night. Nobody wanted to tell us where he
    was. I spotted him, he was outside the
    Kebab shop. He saw us then he ran.

INT CAR.

                    SAMMY
                (Charged on coke)
    Put your fucking foot down he's getting
    away.

Sammy and Marcus laugh as Danny runs for his life.
They anticipate where he is going. He ducks down a
pathway to avoid them. They nearly catch him.

                    MARCUS
                (Swerving around a corner)
    Little fucker's heading towards his house.
    We'll catch him the other side of the
    Parade.

Danny looks as the car drives away. He turns and
runs up an alley. As he gets half way down Sammy
appears at one end, he then turns to see Marcus at
the other end. They slowly close in on him.

                    SAMMY
              (Calling out to Danny)
      We've taken the debt off of Fat Tony Dan.
      Looks like you're in shit street now.

Sammy and Marcus laugh as they close in on a
frightened Danny.

                    MARCUS
            (Throwing Danny against a fence)
      Looks like your gonna have to take a good
      hiding. Maybe then, you might remember to
      pay up on time.

Marcus punches Danny in the face then the stomach,
Danny drops to the floor.

Sammy attacks Danny like a savage, clearly going too
far. Marcus pulls him off and sees the blood stained
knife.

                    MARCUS
                  (Shocked)
      What the fuck have you done Sammy?

                    SAMMY
         (Being carried away by Marcus, shouting
                  back at Danny)
      Do you know who I am?

Danny looks down and sees the amount he is bleeding
and starts to panic.

                    MARCUS
                (To Danny shocked)
      Get yourself home. Now.

                    SAMMY
          (Screaming over Marcus's shoulder)
      You fucking deserve that.

7   INT. MARCUS'S FLAT CONT'D – DAY.   7

Marcus sits with his head down in shame and Vince holds back his anger.

> MARCUS
>
> That's exactly how it happened. We were supposed to just give him a slap and let him know who we were. Sammy was off his head on coke, he always is. His old man makes me look after him, that's the deal. I ain't no murderer. I can't live with that shit.

Marcus looks up at Vince with a tear in his eye.

> VINCE
> *(Calm)*
>
> Would you testify?

Marcus looks confused.

> MARCUS
> *(Nodding and wiping a tear from his eye)*
> Yeah. Yeah I'd testify. The only problem is that even the old bill are in Ronnie's pocket.

> VINCE
> *(Shaking his head)*
> Ronnie's nothing. Charlie's the gov'nor. Are you sure you'd testify?

> MARCUS
> *(Sure)*
> Whenever you're ready.

> VINCE
>
> Go somewhere you can lay low for a while and I'll be in touch. Give me a number I can contact you on and don't make contact with anyone else. We clear?

Vince holds his hand out for Marcus to shake.

> MARCUS
> *(Shaking Vince's hand)*
> Clear. I thought you were gonna kill me.

Marcus looks at Vince relieved.

> VINCE
> *(Pulling him close)*
> I definitely will if you fuck me over.

Out on a nervous Marcus.

8   **INT. SUPERMARKET – DAY.**   8

Freddie and George are making their way around the
supermarket.

> FREDDIE
> *(Holding up some cereal)*
> What about these George, two for one?

> GEORGE
> *(Tired)*
> Yeah, chuck 'em in.

Freddie puts the cereal in and they walk slowly up
one of the aisles.

> FREDDIE
> *(Inquisitive)*
> What do you think Vince is up to?

> GEORGE
> I dunno, but whatever he does he won't do
> half a job.

> FREDDIE
> Do you think Marcus will tell Vince what he
> needs to know?

> GEORGE
> *(Smiling to himself)*
> Your brother is very persuasive when he
> wants to be.

They head past a MAN FACING THE WINES AND SPIRITS.
As they walk past, we reveal that it is DELGADO
looking on.

9   **INT. THE MOON PUB – DAY.**   9

Lenny stands at the bar. Billy sits with a pint.
Vince enters and looks stern.

                         VINCE
                 (Walking around the bar)
         Where's Ronnie?

                         BILLY
                     (Quickly)
         In his office.

Vince doesn't break his stride and heads for the
DOOR marked 'PRIVATE'.

Inside the office Ronnie sits looking at the CC TV
monitor, he sees Vince and braces himself.

Vince bursts through the door and makes for Ronnie.

                         VINCE
         (Throwing Ronnie back into his chair)
         You know why I came back and you know what
         I think of you, right?

                         RONNIE
                  (Under pressure)
         What's going on?

                         VINCE
                      (Firm)
         Your boy has a lot to answer for.

                         RONNIE
                    (Innocent)
         What do you mean?

                         VINCE
                      (Firm)
         He's gone too far and he's gonna pay for
         it.

Vince stands and releases Ronnie.

                         RONNIE
                 (Adjusting himself)
         Pay, how?

                    VINCE
You know how it works Ron, an eye for an
eye.
                    RONNIE
                 (Scared)
He's just a kid Vince.

                    VINCE
Yeah, well you become a man when you take
someone's life in my book.

                    RONNIE
It's the drugs Vinnie, they've got hold of
him. He don't know what he's doin'.

                    VINCE
              (Looking around the room)
You'd better let Charlie know. I'm gonna
bring your little empire down and you know
what they say Ron, the bigger they are the
harder they fall.

Vince heads toward the door and opens it.

                    VINCE (CONT'D)
I'm gonna take care of your boy Ron, one
way or another I'm gonna sort it. You can
tell who you like, they ain't stopping me,
be sure of that. If I can't get to him I'll
be back for you. So make sure next time
you're ready. You and me Ron, we've got
unfinished business.

Vince leaves. Ronnie watches him on the CCTV then
picks the phone up and pauses before putting it back
down. Ronnie puts his head in his hands before
pulling himself together. He stands then drains the
glass of whisky on his desk and puts his coat on.

10   **INT. KEPPEL'S HOUSE – DAY.**   10

Lucy is preparing dinner as the phone rings. She
looks at the display and it reads 'RONNIE MOB' she
answers.
                    LUCY
              (Holding the phone to her ear)
Hello.

SPLIT SCREEN.

                    RONNIE
              (Driving erratically)
     Where's Sammy?

                    LUCY
     He's not in.

                    RONNIE
     Did he say where he was going?

                    LUCY
     Does he ever? What's wrong?

                    RONNIE
     I'm gonna look for him, he might be in
     trouble.

                    LUCY
              (Concerned)
     What sort of trouble Ron? What's going on?

                    RONNIE
              (Worried)
     Vince has got it in his head that Sammy is
     somehow responsible for Danny's death.

                    LUCY
              (Confused)
     Why would he think that? What has Sammy got
     to do with Danny?

                    RONNIE
              (Panicking)
     Don't ask. If he comes home make him wait,
     then ring me. I've tried his mobile and
     Marcus's, their both off. I'm gonna fly
     around Marcus's flat. Ring me if he comes
     home, we've got to get away from here, it's
     all gonna get nasty.

Ronnie hangs up. We stay FULL SCREEN on Lucy as she
ponders for a moment. She picks the phone back up
and dials.

SPLIT SCREEN.

Lenny answers in the pub.

>   LENNY
>   (*Picking the phone up*)
>   Hello The Moon…

>   LUCY
>   (*Cutting in*)
>   Lenny it's me.

>   LENNY
>   Hello Mrs Keppel, Ronnie's…

>   LUCY
>   (*Cutting in*)
>   I need to speak to Vince.

>   LENNY
>   (*Calmly*)
>   Vince? Why are you…

>   LUCY
>   (*Cutting in again*)
>   Lenny please. I need to see Vince and it
>   needs to be between us. Tell him I will
>   meet him 5PM at the church. He'll know
>   where.

>   LENNY
>   (*Calm*)
>   I'll let him know.

>   LUCY
>   (*Upset*)
>   Lenny please don't tell anyone, please I
>   beg you.

>   LENNY
>   I'll sort it, trust me ok, bye-bye.

We stay FULL SCREEN with Lenny as he ponders his
next move.

11   **EXT. MARCUS'S FLAT – DAY.**   11

Ronnie franticly presses the buzzer, the YOUNG
ATTRACTIVE LADY from earlier walks toward the door
with some SHOPPING.

                    RONNIE
                (Facing the lady)
Do you know Marcus?

                  YOUNG LADY
                  (Smiling)
Well he is popular today isn't he.

                    RONNIE
                  (Confused)
What do you mean?

                  YOUNG LADY
        (Getting her keys from her bag)
Some bloke was looking for him earlier.

She opens the door. Ronnie puts his hand across and
holds the door firm blocking her way.

                    RONNIE
                    (Firm)
This bloke, what did he look like?

                  YOUNG LADY
                 (Nervously)
Err, 5' 10 athletic, attractive.

Ronnie walks toward his car in a hurry. He pulls his
phone out and dials.

SPLIT SCREEN.

                  PATTERSON
                 (Answering)
Hello.

                    RONNIE
                  (Stressed)
It's all gone wrong, Vince is on the war
path and I can't find anyone.

                  PATTERSON
                    (Firm)
Calm the fuck down will ya, take a breath
and start from the beginning.

                    RONNIE
              (Gathering himself)
He's going after Sammy, then he said he's
gonna bring us all down.

                  PATTERSON

Did he mention me?

                    RONNIE
What? No but if he comes after me I'll
fucking mention you so don't think your
gonna worm your way out of this.

                  PATTERSON
                 (Alarmed)
Listen calm yourself down and learn some
fucking manners. Who have you looked for?

                    RONNIE
Fat Tony, Marcus and I can't find Sammy
either. What if he's got to Sammy already…

                  PATTERSON
                (Cutting in)
He aint, sort yourself out and think
straight. Don't say anything to Charlie
just yet. Let me make some calls and see
what I can come up with.

                    RONNIE
              (Composing himself)
I'll keep looking for Sammy. If I find him
I'm fucking out of here.

                  PATTERSON
I'll ring you if I hear anything.

They hang up and we stay with Patterson as he dials
another number.

                  PATTERSON
                   (Sly)
Charlie, we need to meet ASAP.

12   INT. NELSON'S FRONT ROOM – DAY.   12

Vince, Freddie and Jack sit at the table while
George serves food. Billy is asleep in the chair.

                    FREDDIE
          What's our next move?

                     VINCE
          I need to talk to Sammy Keppel.

                    FREDDIE
          Do you think he might know something?

                     VINCE
          Yeah, he might do.

                    GEORGE
                  (Sitting)
          And what happens when you find Sammy Keppel
          Vince?

                     VINCE
              (Looking around the table)
          We find out what he knows.

                     JACK
          I'm with you Vince. We all are.

                    GEORGE
                  (Nodding)
          Yeah Jack's right we're with you. But
          within reason.

                     VINCE
          Yeah sure, within reason.

Vince and George exchange a look and it's a look
George knows very well.

The phone rings and Freddie picks it up.

                    FREDDIE
                (Into the phone)
          Hello. Is that you Len? Hold on mate.

Freddie turns to Vince.

                  FREDDIE (CONT'D)
              (Offering the receiver)
          It's for you.

Vince stands and takes the phone still facing the group.

                    VINCE
              (Into the phone)
      Hello (pause) where (Pause) when.

Vince looks at his watch.

                    VINCE (CONT'D)
              (Picking his jacket up)
      I'll be there.

Vince hangs the phone up.

                    VINCE (CONT'D)
              (Heading out)
      I'll be back soon.

The brothers look in wonder.

                    FREDDIE
      Who are you meeting?

                    VINCE
              (Stopping to address the group calmly)
      I'll be back soon.

Vince leaves.

13   **INT. THE MOON PUB – DAY.**   13

Lenny pulls the same crumpled piece of paper from his pocket and dials the number.

                    LENNY
              (Into the phone)
      Hello, erm it's Lenny Hodge again, erm I
      really need to talk to you erm, I'll try
      again later.

Lenny hangs the phone up and looks distressed.

14   **EXT. CANAL WALK – DAY.**   14

Patterson sits on a park bench watching the world go by.

                    CHARLIE (O.C.)
          This better be good.

Patterson turns to see Charlie standing behind him,
his CAR AND DRIVER wait in the background.

                    PATTERSON
                    (Concerned)
          It's about Ronnie.

Charlie slowly walks around the BENCH and starts to
walk along the CANAL.

                    CHARLIE
                    (Not looking back)
          Walk with me.

Patterson stands and takes Charlie's side. Charlie
sets the slow pace.

                    CHARLIE (CONT'D)
                    (Casually)
          What's the problem?

                    PATTERSON
          Ronnie is starting to panic. Vince has
          started to muscle him and his boy. He's
          scared of what Vince might find out.

Charlie looks at Patterson.

                    CHARLIE
                    (Stern)
          What can he find out?

                    PATTERSON
          About Sammy and Danny, you know.

                    CHARLIE
                    (Unphased)
          What about them?

                    PATTERSON
                    (Sarcastically)
          Do you want me to spell it out?

                    CHARLIE
                  (In quick)
Cut your fucking tone, get some fucking
decorum about ya. What I'm saying, who is
gonna say anything to Vince?

                    PATTERSON
                   (Calm)
Vince knows Sammy did it.

                    CHARLIE
Oh, that's a shame. Well he is a bit of a
fucking div anyway.

                    PATTERSON
        (Confused at him having no remorse)
He's your grandson.

Charlie takes a moment to think.

                    CHARLIE
                 (With a plan)
Leave Ronnie to me.

Charlie looks at Patterson's concern.

                  CHARLIE (CONT'D)
What else are you worried about?

                    PATTERSON
Vince ain't gonna stop Charlie. He's got
nothing to lose now.

Charlie stops and slowly turns to Patterson.

                    CHARLIE
Maybe it's time I spoke to Vince.

Charlie looks back to the car and beckons the
driver.

                  CHARLIE (CONT'D)
              (Turning to Patterson)
Keep your end tight and let me handle the
rest.

Patterson looks on as Charlie walks toward the
ADVANCING CAR, the car stops and Charlie leaves not
even acknowledging Patterson.

15   **INT. JUNKIE'S FLAT - DAY.**   15

The CURTAINS ARE DRAWN and the flat is DARK, there
are LINES OF COCAINE with all the obvious
accessories on a table. There are THREE YOUNG MEN
sitting SMOKING A JOINT, Sammy is one of them.

Sammy's phone rings then rings off revealing THIRTY-
SEVEN MISSED CALLS.

               JUNKIE 1
              (Stoned)
   Put it on silent man. It's goin' off every
   fucking minute.

               JUNKIE 2
   Do you owe someone money or something?

The Junkie's giggle, Sammy give's a half smile.

               SAMMY
              (Wasted)
   I don't owe anyone anything. I do my
   own thing, people respect me.

The junkie's share a look then start to giggle.

Sammy is infuriated. He stands, KICKS ONE IN THE
FACE.

Then grabs the other by the scruff of the neck.

             SAMMY (CONT'D)
              (Bitter)
   Fucking funny now is it? Let me tell you
   one thing, nobody fuck's with me. Do you
   understand?

               JUNKIE 2
              (Scared)
   Sorry man sorry, we erm sorry man,
   let me go please Sammy.

The other junkie starts to get up from the floor.
Sammy's eyes are glazed over and his teeth are
clenched.

                    SAMMY
              (Walking out of the flat)
        You lot are prick's.

Sammy kicks the TV over.

                    SAMMY
                  (Leaving)
        Fucking pricks.

16   **INT. NELSON'S HOUSE – DAY.**   16

George and Billy are sitting in the living room, the
TV is off and they sit in silence.

                    BILLY
              (Breaking the silence)
        He knows what he's doing.

                    GEORGE
              (Putting his head in his hands)
        I hope so Bill.

                    BILLY
        I think he's out for more than justice for
        Danny.

                    GEORGE
                (Lifting his head)
        What do you mean?

                    BILLY
                  (Settling)
        He's always maintained his innocence.

George knows what Billy is referring too.

                    GEORGE
                    (In)
        Yeah. What's your point?

                    BILLY
        Well, if he is innocent, then someone
        ain't.

                    GEORGE
Do you think he has a point to prove then?

                    BILLY
Yeah definitely. Whoever got him nicked
that night put him behind bars when Dad
died. They never let him out for the
funeral, that fucking killed him. And
losing Mum. Well let's just say I wouldn't
want to be them right about now, you know
what he's like.

                    GEORGE
                  (Caring)
He's a good man Bill.

                    BILLY
                  (Agreeing)
Oh yeah no doubts. But he's a nasty
bastard.

Out on a worried George and Billy.

17   **EXT. GRAVEYARD - EVENING.**   17

Vince stands over his PARENT'S GRAVE alone. His
serenity is broken.

                    LUCY (O.C.)
Hello Vince.

Vince turns to see Lucy standing ten or so feet
away, he turns to face her.

                    VINCE
                  (Firm)
I know why you wanted to see me. He's done
wrong Lucy, I've got to do something.

She slowly walks to Vince.

                    LUCY
                  (Calm)
Let me talk Vince, at least give me that.

                    VINCE
                 (Bitter)
It's a shame you never wanted to do that
twenty years ago, things might have been
different.

Vince turns his back on her and takes a couple of
paces towards his parent's grave. He looks down at
the stone tablet. Lucy appears over his shoulder.

                VINCE (CONT'D)
                 (Emotional)
I've got to sort this out. I'm sorry Lucy,
but nothing you've got to say can change my
mind.

                    LUCY
                 (Softly)
He's yours Vince.

Vince takes this in for a moment, then turns to face
Lucy.

                LUCY (CONT'D)
He's your son.

                    VINCE
                (Confused)
Nah. No way. You're just trying to protect
him. That's cheap Lucy.

Vince turns away again, Lucy OTS.

                    LUCY
I found out when you were arrested. By the
time I knew, we had stopped all contact. I
was scared.

Vince turns to face Lucy.

                    VINCE
            (Angry, but controlled)
We? What do you mean we? I tried everything
possible to contact you. You never wanted
to know.

                    LUCY
It wasn't as easy as that, things were
difficult.

                    VINCE
Difficult for who? I was nicked for
something your husband done.

                    LUCY
Stop it Vince, I don't want to hear your
lies.

                    VINCE
Lies? That's classy coming from you. You
just told me Sammy's my son.

                    LUCY
                 (Calming)
He is Vince, I'm not lying. Just hear me
out, please.

Vince calms.

                    VINCE
Let's walk, I can't do this here.

Vince and Lucy start to walk away from the grave
toward the CANAL.

                    LUCY
It's hard to know where to start really.

She takes a breath then relaxes. Vince is obviously
smitten with her.

                    LUCY (CONT'D)
We were together for a long time Vince,
nearly six years. I thought that was it, me
and you forever.

Vince looks hurt but stern.

                    LUCY (CONT'D)
My father was always against us and that
was hard. He always insisted you were no
good. The night you got arrested, seemed to
prove him right. I didn't want to believe

it, but how could I not. He told me not to
make contact and had people watching my
every move. To be honest Vince I was
distraught. I thought I knew you.

                    VINCE
You never gave me a chance to explain.

                    LUCY
What would you of said? You were innocent.

                    VINCE
I was.

                    LUCY
That would have confused me even more.
After a few weeks I found out I was
pregnant. I didn't know where to turn.

She stops and looks directly at Vince.

                LUCY (CONT'D)
                  (Softly)
Could you imagine if I'd of told my Dad I
was carrying your child? That would have
been it. He would have made me get rid of
him, no two ways about it.

                    VINCE
            (Clutching at straws)
You could of run away.

                    LUCY
Where Vince, I was just a kid myself.

                    VINCE
You could of gone to my house, my Dad would
of looked out for you.

                    LUCY
Could you imagine what hell my Dad would of
put your family knowing you weren't about
to protect them.

Vince knows the answer. They continue to walk.

                    VINCE
Who else knew?

                    LUCY
My friend Karen, that was it and she moved
away shortly after.

                    VINCE
Why Ronnie, how did all that come about?

                    LUCY
              (Slightly embarrassed)
Ronnie started to do bits for my Dad, so he
was around the house a lot. Karen thought
she was doing the right thing by telling
him.

Vince stops Lucy.

                    VINCE
Wait a minute, Ronnie knew? Ronnie knows?

                    LUCY
              (Embarrassed)
Yeah, Ronnie knows.

                    VINCE
              (Angry)
Why didn't he tell me, he was supposed to
be my mate.

                    LUCY
Ronnie knew how my Dad felt about you and I
told him what he would make me do if he
found out about the baby.

                    VINCE
              (Realizing)
So Ronnie let everyone think that the baby
was his so he could worm his way in. He
always had a thing for you.

                    LUCY
I was scared Vince, I agreed, so we told my
Dad.

                    VINCE
Makes perfect sense. He gets a grandchild
and a son in law he can control, the
perfect little family.

Vince turns and stands facing the canal in disgust,
Lucy OTS.

                    LUCY
                   (Hurt)
        Please don't be too hard, I did what I
        thought was right.

Vince turns to face her.

                    VINCE
        Right, for who? I was behind bars going
        fucking insane. I tried and tried to
        contact you but nothing. Then my brother
        tells me you're with Ronnie. Can you
        imagine how I felt?

                    LUCY
        I'm sorry Vince.

Vince turns away again, Lucy OTS.

                    VINCE
        Yeah, you're not the only one.

Lucy looks hurt.

                    LUCY
        The reason I wanted to keep the baby so
        much is because I loved you. If I couldn't
        have you, then I wanted a part of you that
        nobody could take away from me.

Vince faces her.

                    VINCE
                   (Softening)
        If you felt that way why didn't you answer
        my letters, or my calls? My brothers told
        you I needed to see you but you just
        dropped me.

                    LUCY
        For years my father told me you were no
        good and that you weren't the angel you
        came across as. After the robbery, I began
        to think he was right.

                    VINCE
                   (In)
He was wrong Lucy. I was never meant to be
there that night.

Lucy is willing to listen. Vince slowly start's to
walk as Lucy takes his side.

                VINCE (CONT'D)
I was at home that night making Freddie
something to eat when the phone rang…

18   INT. F/B NELSON'S HOUSE - NIGHT.   18

A twenty-year-old Vince is standing at the cooker
making beans on toast for a five-year-old Freddie
who is sitting at the kitchen table impatiently. The
phone rings.

                    VINCE
             (Trying to multi task)
Who the fuck rings this time of night?

Vince glances at the clock it reads 23:38. He puts
the pan back on the stove and looks for the phone.

                   FREDDIE
             (Jestingly taunting)
You said fuck, you said fuck, you said
fuck.

Vince turns to Freddie as the phone stops.

                    VINCE
No Fred, come on mate turn that in.

A sixteen-year-old Jack opens the door and indicates
that there is a phone call.

                    JACK
           (Around the living room door)
Lenny's on the phone. What's he still doing
up?

                    VINCE
             (Almost relived)
Don't ask, he'ar finish that off.

Vince passes a tea towel and spoon to Jack as he
moves into the kitchen. We follow Vince into the
front room. Vince picks the phone up.

SPLIT SCREEN.

                    VINCE
          Hello Len.

                    LENNY
                 (Panicking)
          Vince, Ronnie's in trouble. He's broken
          into the warehouse where they keep all the
          fags, he's in there now. What shall I do?
          He's gonna get nicked?

                    VINCE
          I'll meet you there.

19   **EXT. GRAVEYARD CONT'D – EVENING.**   19

Vince and Lucy are sitting on a park bench.

                    VINCE
          By the time I got there, Ronnie was nowhere
          to be seen…

20   **INT/EXT. F/B WAREHOUSE – NIGHT.**   20

Vince arrives. THE TRADE DOOR OF THE WAREHOUSE HAS
BEEN FORCED OPEN. Vince looks around then enters.

Once inside he cautiously moves to the CAGES OF
CIGARETTES.

                    VINCE
                 (Calling out)
          Hello. Hello. Ronnie.

Vince looks down to see an UNCONSCIOUS SECURITY
GUARD IN A POOL OF BLOOD. There is a SHOTGUN lying
on the ground next to him.

                    VINCE (CONT'D)
                 (Panicking)
          Fucking hell.

Vince kneels to attend to the guard then picks up the shotgun. The guard is in a bad way.

Someone SHINES A TORCH at Vince. It's the POLICE, Vince drops the shotgun and raises his hands.

> POLICE OFFICER
> *(From a distance, calling firm)*
> Stay where you are, don't move.

FIFTEEN POLICE enter the building. Vince is thrown to the floor and handcuffed.

SLOW MOTION.

Vince is dazed. He looks up to see a young Patterson being commended by his superior. Patterson smiles and looks at Vince.

21 **EXT. GRAVEYARD CONT'D - EVENING.**   21

Lucy is engrossed. She believes him as she wipes a tear from her eye.

> VINCE
> *(Finishing off)*
> …the rest you know.

They sit in silence as Lucy takes it all in.

> VINCE (CONT'D)
> *(Turning to face her)*
> I'm innocent Luce.

She nods in agreement.

> LUCY
> *(With feeling)*
> I'm so sorry Vince.

He stands to hide his emotion.

> VINCE
> *(Shrugging it off)*
> Yeah well it's done now.

Lucy stands opposite Vince and they look at each other wondering what could have been.

Vince brings himself together and gets back on track. He walks to the canal edge and looks into space.

                    VINCE (CONT'D)
          Sammy's done wrong Luce.

                    LUCY
          Please Vince help him. Help him sort his
          life out. Don't punish him.

                    VINCE
          Are you gonna tell him? I mean about me.
          Are you gonna tell him about me?

                    LUCY
          It's gonna change everything.

                    VINCE
          Everything has already changed.

She looks at him waiting for guidance.

                    VINCE (CONT'D)
          Are you gonna tell him?

                    LUCY
                 (Defeated)
          Yeah. I'll tell him. But please don't hurt
          Ronnie.

                    VINCE
                 (Turning his back on her)
          I can't promise you that.

Vince turns to face her. They move in very intimately, she is smitten as is he.

                    VINCE (CONT'D)
          I'm sorry Luce.

They share a look then Vince moves off as she watches him leave.

HIGH WIDE SHOT.

CREDITS ROLL.

REFLECTION: CLOSING MONOLOGUE

That's not what I expected, definitely not how I thought it would go. I have to do some serious thinking, how do I deal with this now? As I said, things have already changed. Something tells me that there are a few more surprises around the corner. Things are going to get interesting that is for sure.

FADE TO BLACK.

END OF EPISODE 4.

Episode 5

Rough justice

INTRODUCTION: OPENING MONOLOGUE

Sometimes in life you have to make choices and no one ever said it would be easy. I have so many emotions and questions right now, some I know I'll get answers to and some, well, I'm not sure I want. What I have been told changes the game. How much? Who knows? I still have to seek justice for my brother, but at what cost? This is what we are about to find out.

The harder the conflict, the greater the triumph – George Washington

1   **INT. LENNY'S BEDSIT – MORNING.**   1

Lenny sits unhappily in the armchair. He is watching
breakfast TV and eating toast, wearing an old vest.
The place is a mess.

A knock at the door breaks his concentration. Lenny
gets up and opens the door to reveal DS Delgado.

> LENNY
> *(Showing him in)*

Come in.

Delgado looks at the state of the place as Lenny
moves some dirty clothes from a chair so Delgado can
sit.

> LENNY (CONT'D)
> *(Offering a chair)*

Take a seat.

> DELGADO
> *(Politely)*

I'll stand thanks Lenny. I'm glad you
called, we knew we could trust you.

Lenny smiles uncomfortably in embarrassment.

> DELGADO (CONT'D)
> *(Looking out of the window at the rundown area)*

We can look after you Lenny. If the
information you are about to give us is
useable, we can make sure nobody can get to
you. The NCA are very powerful, you will be
safe.

> LENNY
> *(Embarrassed)*

What if they find out what I'm doin'?

> DELGADO
> *(Calming)*

Look, we've been after them for a long
time. With your information linking the two
of them, we can ensure they both get what
they deserve.

                    LENNY
              (Hanging his head)
I've seen what they can do, it's not
pretty. If they find out I'm even talking
to you they would have me killed.

                    DELGADO
                (Reassuring)
Look Lenny, you've been loyal for a long
time. I promise you they won't even worry
about what you are up to until it's too
late. We will protect you. At the moment
this is an informal chat, that's all. You
know, like you'd have with anyone.

                    LENNY
                  (Sharp)
Please, don't patronize me. I'm not a
fucking idiot.

                    DELGADO
               (To the point)
Lenny we need those discs. If they hold the
information you say they do, you have
nothing to worry about. You will be safe, I
give you my word. I can't stress how
important you are to this investigation.

                    LENNY
       (Closing his eyes almost praying)
The other thing I told you about, you know
the thing that happened a long time ago.

                    DELGADO
Yeah, what about it?

                    LENNY
What will happen about that?

                    DELGADO
If the confession is on one of the discs,
Vince will probably be given a pardon. But,
the confession will definitely add to the
other's sentences.

Delgado puts his hand on an emotional Lenny's
shoulder.

                          DELGADO
          You're doing the right thing Lenny.

Out on Lenny's CU.

2   **EXT. STREET – MORNING.**   2

Vince walks along the street in-between the tower
blocks on an estate.

A car quickly screeches' up in front of him. He
stops. Four heavies in the car look at Vince. He
looks back.

                       VINCE (POV)
          What do you want?

WE HEAR A THUD AND THE SCREEN IMMEDIATELY TURNS
BLACK.

3   **INT. EMPTY FLAT – DAY.**   3

VINCE POV - FROM BLACK TO BLUR TO FOCUS, we can hear
voices but it's inaudible as Vince comes around.

Vince is laying on the floor with his hands CABLE
TIED behind his back.

He tries to struggle but quickly gives up. He tries
to make it to his feet and nearly does. He is kicked
to the floor again.

                       HEAVY 1
                 (Hard, standing over Vince)
          That looked like it hurt.

Vince looks around to face the thug.

                       VINCE
          Who put you up to this?

Vince is lifted to his feet by his hair. Once he is
upright, he counts out four heavies.

                       HEAVY 1
                 (Calling to the next room)
          He's up Guv.

Vince watches in anticipation to see who appears through the doorway. A LARGE SIX-FOOT PLUS distinguished looking man walks in and stands in front of Vince.

> LINCOLN
> Hello Vincent. I'm sure you're wondering who I am. My name is Lincoln, and I work for Mr Madigan. Charlie Madigan, I'm sure you know him.

Lincoln moves in, now nose to nose with Vince while two of the thugs hold him still.

> LINCOLN (CONT'D)
> (Smarmy)
> He doesn't like you very much does he? Now what could you of done that has pissed him off that much that he called me?

Vince says nothing.

> LINCOLN (CONT'D)
> (Looking Vince up and down)
> I'll be honest, you don't look much.

> VINCE
> Untie me and we'll find out. Its Vince by the way.

Lincoln sarcastically laughs and moves away. He walks around the room slowly, still talking to Vince.

> LINCOLN
> (Mocking)
> I could eat more than you for breakfast son.

> VINCE
> Well, you've got a good appetite then ain't ya.

Nose to nose with Vince again.

> LINCOLN
> (Intrigued)
> Yeah. I have.

Lincoln punches Vince in the stomach. Vince
drops to the ground. Lincoln then kicks him
in the back for good measure.

                    LINCOLN (CONT'D)
                       (Cocky)
          Mr Madigan said you were a handful.
          (Smug)
          Pussy.

Lincoln signals for the heavies to pick Vince up,
they oblige. As he gets to his feet, Charlie walks
in and makes his way over to Vince.

                    CHARLIE
          Hello Vincent. I mean Vince. I take it my
          associates have been welcoming?

Vince just looks at him in disgust.

                    CHARLIE (CONT'D)
          I'm sure you're wondering why you're here.

                    VINCE
          Not really.

                    CHARLIE
               (Sarcastically smiling)
          Always were too big for your boots weren't
          ya boy.

Vince glares at Charlie.

                    CHARLIE (CONT'D)
          I hear your thinking of going after my
          grandson?

Charlie takes a deep intake of breath, and then
faces Vince.

                    CHARLIE (CONT'D)
          Big mistake Vince. Very big mistake.

                    VINCE
          He's done wrong, and you fucking know it.

                    CHARLIE
                     (In)
     Vincent Vincent, Vincent. We're all guilty
     of doing wrong. We've all done things we
     regret, you know, silly things.

Charlie paces around Vince, Vince raises his
eyebrows at the Vincent comment.

                    CHARLIE (CONT'D)
     Now to be honest Vince, I wouldn't believe
     everything you hear. People say things to
     get themselves out of shit. Sometimes its
     barefaced fucking lies.

Turns to face Vince.

                    CHARLIE (CONT'D)
                   (Smiling)
     Know what I mean?

Charlie paces.

                    CHARLIE (CONT'D)
     That fucking gutless arsehole Marcus. Now
     he talked out of school didn't he? Fucking
     lied to save himself, and then the cheeky
     bastard asked me to help him.

Turns to face Vince.

                    CHARLIE (CONT'D)
     Oh, I fucking helped him alright. Grassed
     my grandson up to save himself, some
     fucking people.

Charlie paces.

                    CHARLIE (CONT'D)
     Now I have another problem. Ronnie. Looks
     like Ronnie wants to run his mouth off and
     fuck things up for me as well.

Turns to face Vince.

                    CHARLIE (CONT'D)
                   (Smug)
     Now we can't have that, can we Vince?

                    VINCE
        Do me a favor Charlie. Fuck off.

Charlie nods to the heavies who are enforcing the
situation. Lincoln punches Vince in the face cutting
his lip and nose.

Charlie paces.

                    CHARLIE
        Now, where was I? Oh yeah Ronnie.

Charlie lights a cigar.

                    CHARLIE (CONT'D)
        You, Ronnie and Lenny were best mates at
        one stage weren't ya? What went wrong?

Charlie faces Vince.

                    CHARLIE (CONT'D)
                  (Sarcastic)
        Oh yeah, you got yourself nicked.

Charlie paces.

                    CHARLIE (CONT'D)
        Do you ever wonder about that night Vince?

Lincoln prompts Vince to answer.

                    VINCE
        What about it?

Charlie faces Vince.

                    CHARLIE
        The phone call from Lenny, the shotgun, no
        Ronnie. All of it.

                    VINCE
        Why are you telling me this? What you
        trying to say?

                    CHARLIE
        Come on Vince you ain't that fucking stupid
        are you? You're out the way, Ronnie gets
        the girl. Is the penny starting to drop?

Vince looks angry.

                    CHARLIE (CONT'D)
          All those years you thought you done the
          right thing, took one for your mate, the
          unwritten code and all that shit. And all
          along, you were set up and like a fucking
          idiot you fell for it. Hook, line and
          fucking sinker.

Charlie paces.

                    CHARLIE (CONT'D)
          Funny how Ronnie and Lenny stopped coming
          to see you ain't it? Mates, they played you
          for a fucking fool. Just to get you out the
          way, and you fell for it.

Charlie faces a tormented Vince.

                    CHARLIE (CONT'D)
          Well, it's been nice catching up Vince, but
          I've really got to go now.

Charlie walks over to the door, stops and turns to
face Vince one last time.

                    CHARLIE (CONT'D)
          In case you get any ideas, these lads will
          be sticking around for a bit. You know, to
          look after my best interests.

                    CHARLIE (CONT'D)
                    (To Lincoln)
          Not too much lads, just let him know.

Charlie leaves as Lincoln and the heavies set about
Vince.

4   EXT. GRAVEYARD - DAY.   **4**

George, Frank, Billy and Jack are in the graveyard,
they are standing over the FAMILY GRAVE. George
looks at his watch.

                    GEORGE
          It's twenty past now. They're taking the
          piss. Half-hour that is all I asked.

                    FRANK
             (Checking his phone)
     I've gotta shoot George, I've still got two
     jobs.

George shakes Frank's hand.

                    GEORGE
     Thanks for coming Frank. It's a shame your
     brothers didn't bother.

                    FRANK
          (Putting his hand on George's shoulder)
     I'm sure there is a good reason.

George nods, they say goodbye to Frank. Frank walks
out of the gate and gets into his van.

As he drives off and around the corner LEFT OF FRAME
Freddie runs around the corner RIGHT OF FRAME and
gets to the boys out. He is out of breath and
frantic.

                    BILLY
             (Stopping Freddie)
     Slow down Fred. What's wrong?

Freddie tries to catch his breath.

                    GEORGE
                  (Angry)
     You do know it's Mum's birthday, you was
     meant to…

                    FREDDIE
          (Trying to get his words out)
     It's Vince, he's hurt.

The boys look stunned.

                    JACK
     Come on.

The boys jump into the ROVER and speed off.

5   **INT/EXT. RONNIE'S CAR – DAY.**   5

Ronnie scours the streets looking for Sammy.
Ronnie's car is parked, and the engine is running.
He is talking to a youth.

> RONNIE
> *(Mid-sentence)*
> Well if you do, bell this number. Straight
> away, you understand.

> YOUTH
> Yeah, will do Mr Keppel.

Ronnie pulls off looking either side of the road in
case he sees Sammy.

RONNIE DIALS 'HOME' ON THE HANDS FREE PHONE.

> LUCY
> Hello.

> RONNIE
> It's me, is he home yet?

> LUCY
> No, not yet. I spoke to Vince.

> RONNIE
> *(Angry)*
> What?

> LUCY
> I spoke to Vince.

> RONNIE
> Did he threaten you?

> LUCY
> No, not at all.

> RONNIE
> What did he say?

> LUCY
> He wanted to hurt Sammy.

                    RONNIE
I'm on it. When I find Sammy, we'll fuck
off for a while, until Vince gets sorted.

                    LUCY
Is that what happened last time?

                    RONNIE
What do you mean?

                    LUCY
When Vince was arrested? Did you get that
sorted?

                    RONNIE
You don't know what you're talking about.

                    LUCY
He told me what happened. You was there
that night, in the warehouse.

                    RONNIE
                  (Covering)
He's lying Luce, don't be drawn into it.
He'll say anything to turn you against me.

                    LUCY
He looked very convincing.

                    RONNIE
                  (Angry)
Looked? You saw him?

                    LUCY
Yeah, I met him last night.

                    RONNIE
And you only thought to fucking tell me
now.

                    LUCY
You never came home last night. Your phone
was off. In fact, your phone is always off.

                    RONNIE
                    (*Firm*)
Look, we have to get to Sammy before Vince
does.

                    LUCY
I told him.

                    RONNIE
You told him what?

                    LUCY
                    (*Scared*)
I told him about Sammy.

                    RONNIE
                    (*Firm*)
What?

                    LUCY
I told him everything. He deserved to know.

                    RONNIE
                    (*Shouting*)
You fucking stupid slag, you've fucked it
all up, everything.

                    LUCY
                    (*Crying*)
Please Ronnie…

                    RONNIE
You silly bitch, what difference do you
think that will make to a scumbag like
Vince Nelson.

                    LUCY
He's coming for you Ronnie. Not Sammy, he's
coming for you.
                    RONNIE
                    (*Shouting*)
You're fucking dead, I'm gonna fucking kill
you. You fucking bitch.

Ronnie punches the phone until it is obliterated. We
end on a CU of a distraught and desperate Ronnie.

6   INT. THE NELSON'S HOUSE- DAY.   6

The boys arrive home to see a badly beaten Vince on
the sofa. They run to aid him. Everyone is panicking
and fussing over him.

                    GEORGE
                 (Panicking)
     Who did this?

                    VINCE
     Leave it George, it's gone way too far now.

                    GEORGE
     It's got to stop now Vince, before someone
     gets seriously hurt.

                    VINCE
          (Grinning through his pain)
     It's a bit late for that mate.

                    FREDDIE
                 (Concerned)
     I found him sitting on the doorstep.

George looks at him confused.

                    VINCE
     Well I ain't got a key, and I didn't have
     it in me to get through the back window.

Billy goes to the spirits cabinet.

                    BILLY
          (Pouring a very generous whisky)
     Here you are mate. Get this down ya.

Billy offers Vince the whisky.

                    VINCE
               (Holding his side)
     No thanks Bill.

Billy stops in his tracks.

                    BILLY
          (Shrugging his shoulders)
     Oh well, waste not want not.

Billy downs the whisky.

                    JACK
               (Sincere, soft)
    Would you like a cup of that herbal shit?

Vince laughs.

                  VINCE
    For fucks sake will you lot stop fussing.
    I'll be ok in a while. Let me get myself
    together.

                  GEORGE
                (Serious)
    Do you know who done this Vince?

                  VINCE
    Yeah, and I know why.

Vince stands a bit easier rolling his shoulders.

                  VINCE (CONT'D)
    I'm gonna get showered then I need you to
    take me to Lenny's.

Vince looks at jack.

                    JACK
    No problem.

                  FREDDIE
    I'm coming.

                  VINCE
    Not this time Fred. I need you to go to the
    pub and look for someone with Bill.

                  FREDDIE
    Yeah, alright.

Vince leaves the front room.

                  GEORGE
             (To Billy and Freddie)
    Be careful.

George turns to Jack.

                    GEORGE
          Stay with him.

7   INT/EXT. ROVER – DAY.   7

Jack and Vince exit the Nelson's and get into the
rover.

Jack drives, Vince is uneasy.

                    JACK
          Do you want to borrow my phone and let
          Lenny know you're coming?

                    VINCE
          No.

                    JACK
          This is all about Danny, tell me you ain't
          forgotten that.

Vince is emotionless.

                    VINCE
                    (Stern)
          It's about lots of things now Jack.

                    JACK
          Lenny's one of the good one Vince.

                    VINCE
          Is he?

                    JACK
          He's your mate Vince, you grew up together.

                    VINCE
          That was a long time ago.

                    JACK
          I'm coming in with you.

Vince turns to Jack.

                    VINCE
          No, not this time. You wait in the car.

> JACK

I'm a fully gr…

> VINCE
> *(Cutting in angry)*

You'll wait in the fucking car like I said.

Jack is intimidated by Vince's aggression.

> JACK
> *(Sarcastic)*

Ok, we do it your way.

> VINCE
> *(Calm)*

Thank you Jack. It's for the best.

Jack pulls up. They sit in silence for a moment.

> VINCE (CONT'D)

I'll be back in a while, keep the engine running.

Vince gets out, Jack watches him enter a dilapidated building.

8   **INT. LENNY'S BEDSIT – DAY.**   8

Lenny is asleep in the chair. There is a knock on the door.

> LENNY
> *(Getting up, calling out)*

Hang on.

Lenny opens the door. Vince pushes the door open and throws Lenny onto the bed.

> LENNY (CONT'D)
> *(Squirming)*

Vince you're hurting me.

> VINCE
> *(Face to face)*

Shut your mouth Lenny and let me talk. Do you understand!

Lenny nods and his eyes start to well up.

                    VINCE (CONT'D)
                     (Aggressive)
The night I got nicked, was I set up?

Lenny starts to cry, Vince rags him about.

                    VINCE (CONT'D)
     (Pulling his hand back to punch him, shouting)
The night I got nicked, was I set up?

                    LENNY
          (With floods of tears, shouting)
Yes, yes, yes you was set up.

Vince throws Lenny to the floor and gathers himself
while lenny curls up in a ball crying.

                    VINCE
You dirty bastard. Of all the people Len.

Vince lifts Lenny to his feet by his throat.

                    VINCE (CONT'D)
Of all the people Len, I trusted you.

                    LENNY
They made me do it. I had no choice. I
honestly had no choice Vince.

Vince throws Lenny into the chair and stands over
him.
                    VINCE
There's always a choice. I want to know
everything.

A young man enters from the front door.

                    YOUNG MAN
Is everything ok Lenny, we could hear
shouting?

Vince turns to look.

                    LENNY
          (Wiping a tear from his eye)
I'm fine.

                    YOUNG MAN
    I thought I'd…

                     VINCE
                    (Firm)
    Shut the door on your way out.

Vince and the young man exchange a look. The young
man nervously shuts the door as he leaves. Vince
turns to Lenny.

                     LENNY
    I deserve what I get. I never meant to
    betray you Vince.

Vince stands over him emotionless.

                  LENNY (CONT'D)
    I was in the pub that night, you know when
    Charlie ran it…

9   **INT. F/B THE MOON PUB – NIGHT.**   9

Ronnie and Lenny are playing pool. Charlie is
standing at the bar. Charlie gives TWO MEN some
money then walks over to the pool table.

                  LENNY (V.O.)
    I knew something was up when Ronnie asked
    me to stay behind after the pub shut.

Charlie takes a seat at the bar.

                   BARTENDER
              (Putting his coat on)
    That's me Mr Madigan.

Charlie watches the pool match and doesn't break his
focus.

                    CHARLIE
    Yeah, good night. Leave by the back door.

The bartender leaves, Ronnie looks over at Charlie,
Charlie winks.

                    LENNY (V.O.)
     We had about four or five games then the
     phone rang, Charlie took the call. We just
     carried on playing pool. I knew something
     weren't right. After that call he rang
     someone else, it all happened so quick.
     Once he'd finished with that call he came
     over.

                    CHARLIE
                   (Smiling)
     Enjoying yourselves?

                    LENNY
     Yeah thanks Mr Madigan.

Charlie moves around one side of Lenny while Ronnie
closes in from the other.

                    CHARLIE
     There's something I need you to do for me
     young Leonard.

Lenny looks at both men closing in on him.

                    LENNY
                   (Nervously)
     What do you need me to do?

Charlie shows Lenny to a chair and they both stand
over him.

                    LENNY (V.O.)
     They said they'd hurt my Mum. My Mum Vince!

10   INT. LENNY'S BEDSIT CONT'D – DAY.   10

Vince has his back to Lenny looking at a PHOTO of a
young Lenny and a WOMAN IN A WHEELCHAIR.

                    LENNY (CONT'D)
                   (Softly)
     They would have hurt her. How could anyone
     of hurt her Vince?

                    VINCE
     I served time for that Len.

                    LENNY
                    (In)
Don't you think I think about that every
day? Not a day goes by when I'm not
disgusted with myself.

                    VINCE
And that's meant to make me feel better?

                    LENNY
                  (Embarrassed)
By the time I knew what was going on it was
too late. You'd already been nicked.

                    VINCE
You came to see me, why didn't you say
anything then?

                    LENNY
You was inside Vince, who would of
protected me? Who would have protected my
Mum? They asked me to call you, they said
it was a joke. I had no idea.

Lenny waits for a reaction.

                    VINCE
You sold me out Len. You could of said
something, anything.

                    LENNY
They would have hurt her.

Vince can't look at Lenny.

                 LENNY (CONT'D)
When you came back, I knew I had to put it
right. I knew I had the chance to make it
all better. I've done something Vince.

Lenny tries to put his hand on Vince's shoulder,
Vince shrugs his hand off.

                    VINCE
                   (Bitter)
Get your dirty fucking hands off me.

Vince moves away.

                         LENNY
                      (*Panicking*)
         I've put it right Vince, you'll see. You're
         the best mate I've ever had. Say something,
         please.

Vince grabs Lenny by the scruff of the neck and
throws him against the wall.

                         VINCE
                 (*Through gritted teeth*)
         The only reason I ain't killed you is
         because you're a fucking retard.

Vince throws Lenny to the floor.

                       VINCE (CONT'D)
         You're a fucking coward Len. Ronnie's
         right, you've always been the same.

Vince bends to face a cowering Lenny.

                       VINCE (CONT'D)
         The only reason we had you about when we
         were kids is because we felt sorry for ya.
         You're fucking pathetic.

Vince stands by the door.

                       VINCE (CONT'D)
         Your pathetic, you have the brain of a
         fucking child. Look at you.

Lenny sobs, Vince's words hurt him.

HIGH WIDE SHOT of Lenny sobbing against the door.

11   **INT. KEPPEL'S HOUSE – DAY.**   11

Lucy sits anxiously. Sammy enters. Lucy gets to her
feet.

                         LUCY
         Where have you been?

Sammy is on a downer after his session.

> SAMMY

Out.

> LUCY

We've been worried.

Sammy ignores her and makes his way to his bedroom.

> LUCY (CONT'D)
> (Following)

Sammy, I'm talking to you.

Sammy enters his bedroom and starts to throw clothes
into a HOLD ALL.

> LUCY (CONT'D)
> (Franticly)

Wait.

Sammy slows down ready to listen.

> SAMMY

This better be good.

Sammy sits as Lucy prepares to tell him who his real
father is.

12   **INT. THE MOON PUB – EVENING.**   12

The pub is empty. Billy and Freddie sit at the bar.
Five heavies enter and make their way to the bar.

Billy and Freddie exchange a look. Lincoln fits the
description Vince gave them.

Freddie rings Jack.

SPLITSCREEN.

> JACK
> (Holding the phone to his ear)

Hello.

> BILLY
> (Sure)

There here.

> JACK
> Ring Frank, I'll pick George up.

OUT ON BILLY.

13   INT/EXT. STREET – EVENING.   13

DS Delgado sits in his car. Lenny gets in.

> LENNY
> *(Sitting)*
> I'm sorry I'm late.

> DELGADO
> I thought you had blown me out.

> LENNY
> I had a few ends to tie up.

> DELGADO
> Have you got the discs?

Lenny reaches into his pocket and produces a carrier
bag containing the discs. He hands them to Delgado.

> LENNY
> They are all there.

Delgado takes hold of them, but Lenny still has a
firm grip on them.

> LENNY (CONT'D)
> Make sure.

> DELGADO
> Trust me Lenny, it's done.

Lenny lets go of the discs, Delgado puts them safely
into the door panel.

> DELGADO (CONT'D)
> I'll take you to the safe house and from
> there we…

> LENNY
> *(Cuts in)*
> I've got something I need to do first. I'll
> see you again when I'm ready.

> DELGADO
> What? We'll take you straight into
> protective custody, all…

> LENNY
> *(Cuts in)*
> I'll be fine for now. I need to do this.

> DELGADO
> Arrests are going to be made right now, you
> will be named Lenny.

> LENNY
> *(Un-phased)*
> I know, I'll be in touch.

Lenny gets out and walks off, Delgado watches him.

14   INT. THE MOON PUB CONT'D – NIGHT.   14

The JUKEBOX plays loudly on throughout.

The HEAVIES sit at a table near Billy and Freddie.
Vince, Frank, George and Jack enter.

Lincoln sees Vince and puts his hand inside his
jacket to reach for a GUN.

CU Vince looking at Lincoln.

Freddie kicks Lincoln in the chest, the GUN fly's
across the bar.

Billy hits heavy 1. Heavy 2 punches Freddie, Vince,
Frank and George join the fight.

George and Freddie tackle heavy 2, Billy fights
heavy 1, Jack tackles heavy 3 and Frank throws heavy
4 against the wall.

Vince makes a beeline for Lincoln. We follow Vince
as he picks Lincoln up from the floor by the scruff
of the neck. Nose to nose.

                        VINCE
          I hope you're fucking hungry?

Vince punches Lincoln across the pool table. Lincoln
gets up only to be greeted by Vince coming at him
with a flurry of punches.

We pick up each brother fighting, punches flying.

Freddie and George are doing their best but
struggling.

Frank is well in control as is Jack.

We pan across to Billy as he bites the nose of heavy
1, heavy 1 screams.

Vince and Lincoln exchange punches as we see a
frightened bartender pick the PHONE up to dial a
number, George takes the receiver from him and
smashes heavy 2 in the face.

The scene is like an old-fashioned western.

Heavy 2 punches George to the floor while Freddie
continues to fight.

Frank, Jack and Billy are finishing their fights
off.

Lincoln hits Vince in the ribs, Vince drops to the
ground. Lincoln picks Vince up by the scruff of the
neck and lays him out onto the bar.

                        LINCOLN
                   (Covered in blood)
          Like I said. Pussy.

Vince looks up at him.

                        VINCE

          My baby brother won't be happy with you
          calling me that.

                    LINCOLN
                  (Smiling)
     Tell him to look me up.

Vince holds his ribs. Lincoln pulls his clenched
fist back ready to punch Vince.

VINCE'S EYES FLICK QUICKLY TO THE RIGHT.

                    VINCE
                  (Smirking)
     Tell him yourself.

Lincoln turns to see what Vince has seen, Freddie
nearly takes his head off with a straight right, and
Lincoln drops to the floor.

Freddie and Frank help Vince to his feet. Jack and
Billy help George to his feet.

The brothers stand looking around at the carnage
they have caused.

Jack picks the GUN up.

                    JACK
     I'll take that.

The brothers look at him as they make their way to
the door.

                    JACK (CONT'D)
     What? I'll hand it in later.

The brothers share the moment.

                    JACK (CONT'D)
               (Tucking it into his trousers)
     What? should I of left it there for them
     then?

CU on Freddie helping Vince out the door.

                    VINCE
                  (Proud)
     Not bad Fred, not bad at all. Remind me not
     to piss you off.

                          FREDDIE
                     (Smiling proudly)
          No chance.

They leave. The bartender just stands and looks
around at the heavies as they groan on the floor.

15   **EXT. ALLEY - NIGHT.**   15

Ronnie paces anxiously.

                     CHARLIE (O.C.)
          What do you want?

Ronnie turns to see Charlie silhouetted at the end
of the alley.

                          RONNIE
                     (Walking toward him)
          Thanks for coming.

                          CHARLIE
                          (In)
          That's far enough, make it quick.

                          RONNIE
                     (Close to tears)
          I need your help.

                          CHARLIE
                          (Hard)
          Get hold of yourself man, look at you.
          You're a fucking bumbling wreck.

                          RONNIE
          It's all on top, I need to lie low.

Charlie takes a moment.

                          CHARLIE
          Book into a hotel tonight, and sort
          yourself the fuck out. Meet me at the brick
          yard first thing in the morning.
          (Sarcastic)
          Inside the building Ronnie, out of sight,
          we go from there.

                    RONNIE
     Thank you Charlie.

                    CHARLIE
     No contact with anyone.

Charlie throws Ronnie against the wall.

                  CHARLIE (CONT'D)
     Anyone, you hear me!

                    RONNIE
                  (Desperate)
     Yeah, got it, anyone.

Charlie lets go then straightens Ronnie's collar.

                    CHARLIE
     Give me your mobile Ronnie.

                    RONNIE
     What?

                    CHARLIE
                  (Stern)
     Give me your phone. I just need to make
     sure.

                    RONNIE
             (Giving the phone to Charlie)
     What's gonna happen Charlie?

                    CHARLIE
                  (Casually)
     I'm gonna sort it, like I always do.

                    RONNIE
     Yeah, like you always do.

Charlie slowly walks away.

                    CHARLIE
     Be there by nine.

Ronnie checks his pocket. He has a second phone.

16   INT. LENNY'S BEDSIT – NIGHT.   16

Lenny waits anxiously. There is a knock on the door.
Lenny opens it to reveal billy.

> LENNY
> *(Showing him in)*
> What happened to you?

> BILLY
> *(Looking around)*
> One too many, you know me Len. What's so
> important you wanted me around now,
> couldn't it of waited?

> LENNY
> No, it couldn't.

Lenny sits. Billy perches against the table then
wipes his hand clean.

> LENNY
> Things are going on Bill. I don't know how
> much you know but, well I want you to give
> this to Vince.

Lenny hands Billy an envelope.

> BILLY
> *(Curious)*
> What is it?

> LENNY
> *(Turning his back on Billy)*
> It'll explain everything.

> BILLY
> *(None the wiser)*
> Like what?

> LENNY
> *(Desperate)*
> Please Billy, just make sure he gets it.

Lenny looks tired and weak.

> BILLY
> No problem Len. Is there anything I can do?

> LENNY
> *(Ushering him to the door)*
> That's all Bill. Thank you.

Lenny opens the door. Billy walks out then turns to see Lenny.

> BILLY
> We are here for you Len.

> LENNY
> *(Weary smile)*
> Thanks Bill, God bless you mate.

Out on a concerned Billy.

17   **EXT. OFF-LICENCE – NIGHT.**   17

Patterson walks out unwrapping a packet of CIGARETTES.

SCO19 SWOOP. Patterson is thrown to the floor.

> PATTERSON
> *(Stunned)*
> What the fuck is going on?

Patterson is held face down.

> DELGADO (O.C.)
> You're under arrest on suspicion of
> supplying class A drugs, money laundering,
> perverting the course of justice and
> conspiracy to commit armed robbery. Along
> with might I add, conspiracy to murder.

Patterson turns his head to see who is reading him his rights. DS Delgado walks into view and crouches to make eye contact with Patterson.

> PATTERSON
> *(Held to the floor)*
> You, why? Who are you?

> DELGADO
> *(Casually)*
> I'm with DPS. We've been investigating you
> for a very long time now.

> PATTERSON

You've got nothing on me.

> DELGADO
> *(Sure)*

Oh yes we have. Every meeting you, Ronnie
Keppel and Charlie Madigan have ever had is
on tape. You'll have plenty of time to go
through the evidence.

HIGH WIDE SHOT.

OUT ON PATTERSON BEING TAKEN AWAY.

18   **INT. VINCE'S BEDROOM – NIGHT.**   18

Vince lays on the bed in a bit of agony there is a
knock on the door.

> VINCE
> *(Still laying)*

Come in.

Billy enters sheepishly, still in his jacket.

> VINCE (CONT'D)
> *(Looking over)*

Where have you been?

Billy walks over to Vince.

> BILLY

I've been to see Lenny.

> VINCE
> *(Hard)*

Oh yeah, what did he tell ya.

> BILLY
> *(Soft)*

Not as much as I'd like to know really. He
gave me this though.

Billy offers Vince the envelope, Vince looks the
other way.

                    BILLY (CONT'D)
                (Dropping the envelope on the bed)
For what it's worth, I think you should
read it. You at least owe him that.

                    VINCE
                    (Snapping)
You don't know what you're talking about, I
owe him nothing.

Billy slowly walks to the door.

                    BILLY
                    (Cool)
Yeah. Whatever you say Vince. We're all cut
from the same cloth mate. You don't mean
that, you know it and I know it.

Billy waits a moment, Vince does not reply.

                    BILLY (CONT'D)
Well, it's there when you're ready.

Billy exits leaving Vince lying alone. Vince looks
over at the door then picks the letter up. He opens
it. It reads.

FROM CU OF THE LETTER, SLOWLY TO A HIGH WIDE SHOT.

                    LENNY (V.O.)
Dearest Vince, I've got so much to tell
you. I will start with the fact that you
honestly were the closest thing to a
brother I ever had. You have no idea how
special that made me feel.

19   INT. LENNY'S BEDSIT – NIGHT.   **19**

HIGH WIDE SHOT. Lenny sits alone crying.

                    LENNY (V.O. CONT'D)
Growing up I felt untouchable, safe, as if
nobody could touch me. That night, I had no
idea I was setting you up. I thought I was
doing it as a laugh, to get you out of the
house that late at night for nothing, to
get you at it. Imagine how I felt when I
found out the truth, imagine how I felt

when I found out you'd been nicked. They
threatened me Vince, threatened my Mum God
bless her, you know yourself I'm not the
strongest of people. All I've ever done in
my life is fail, and I failed you. After
all you done for me I never even had the
courage to stand up for you. I've lived
with that guilt for twenty years. Twenty
years guilt ridden and alone, bullied and
taken for granted. Not anymore, I've
finally made a stand, I've done something
about it. I can't live with that guilt
anymore. I've given the old bill enough
evidence to bury all of them, Charlie,
Ronnie even Patterson. Like I said before,
I love you Vince, like a brother. Please
don't think I'm weak for what I'm about to
do. Please find it in your heart to forgive
me. Always your brother. Lenny.

Throughout the narration, Lenny sits and cries in
the chair, he stands and turns the TV off. Lenny
takes a deep breath then pulls a BOWIE KNIFE from
the draw. He slowly sits and pours himself a
generous whisky as if to numb his pain. He cries as
he drinks. Lenny holds the blade to his wrist. The
camera pans from Lenny onto the PHOTO of him and his
mother. We hear him collapse. The CAMERA SLOWLY
TRACKS BACK to a HIGH WIDE SHOT as Lenny tries to
get to his feet then collapses again in a heap on
the floor, he lays motionless. A pool of blood
slowly appears from under his lifeless body.

HIGH WIDE SHOT.

CREDITS ROLL.

CREDITS ROLL.

REFLECTION: CLOSING MONOLOGUE

There are things I think we all learn to live with over the
years, regrets? definitely some. Certainly things that we are
not proud of, that's a fact. Sometimes in life, bad things
happen to good people, that's just how it works. Although, we
all have a choice on how we deal with things, not sometimes,
every time. Let me tell you something right now, my conscience
is clear for the things that I have done in my life, I'm sure
of this. When this is all over, my conscience will still be
clear. No matter what.

FADE TO BLACK.

END OF EPISODE 3.

211

Episode 6

Dead man walking

INTRODUCTION: OPENING MONOLOGUE

Things are slowly getting sorted. It's been a whirlwind so far, not sure who to trust, who to believe and not sure what my next move will be. One thing's for certain, this is where it ends.

Men do not shape destiny, destiny produces the man for the hour – Fidel Castro

1   **INT. NELSON'S KITCHEN – DAY.**   1

Vince sits at the kitchen table reading the
NEWSPAPER. George stands at the sink washing up.

THE PHONE RINGS.

                        GEORGE
    Get that for me.

Vince stands and picks up the phone.

George looks on curiously.

                        VINCE
                  (Into the phone)
    Hello (pause) yeah it's me (pause) yeah,
    when?

Vince does not waste any time. He drains his cup and
puts his coat on. George continues to wash up.

                        GEORGE
                    (Worried)
    Who was that?

                        VINCE
                (Walking out the door)
    See you later.

Vince shuts the door.

                        GEORGE
                (Almost to himself)
    Be careful.

George worries and the effects are starting to show.

Freddie walks into the kitchen.

                        FREDDIE
                (Putting the kettle on)
    Where's Vince gone this early?

George pulls himself together.

> GEORGE
> *(Covering)*
Shops. Are you eating?

> FREDDIE
Yeah, cheers.

Freddie picks up the NEWSPAPER and sits where Vince sat.

Out on George looking at a nonchalant Freddie.

2   **INT. LENNY'S BEDSIT - DAY.**   2

HIGH WIDE SHOT.

The scene is busy with FORENSICS, POLICE and PARAMEDICS.

Forensics gather evidence while a WPC interviews the young man from episode 5 scene 8.

The BODY BAG is zipped up, and taken away.

3   **INT/EXT. BRICKYARD - DAY.**   3

Ronnie is in the derelict building adjacent to the BRICK YARD.

The building is in ruins with rubble on the floor and the windows smashed out, it is open but secluded.

CU RONNIE'S WATCH READS 09:12.

> VINCE (O.C.)
Hello Ronnie.

Ronnie's face changes in recognition. He knows that voice only too well. He realises he has been set up. He turns to face Vince.

Without a word Vince slowly walks toward Ronnie. Ronnie slowly backs up.

Vince breaks the awkward silence as Ronnie gets to the wall and can go no further.

                    VINCE (CONT'D)
     What did I ever do to you?

                         RONNIE
                      (Nervously)
     Come on mate.
                         VINCE
                      (Disgusted)
     Did I deserve it?

                         RONNIE
                      (Ashamed)
     No. No you didn't.

Ronnie eases as he comes to terms with the
situation.

                         VINCE
     You knew about the baby and said nothing.
     Then to top it off you set me up. Why? I
     had nothing anyone could have possibly
     wanted that bad, did I?

Ronnie relaxes a little too much.

                         RONNIE
                     (Comfortable)
     It's not a case of…

Vince punches Ronnie firmly in the stomach
reinforcing his intentions. Ronnie drops to the
floor at Vince's feet.

                         VINCE
     All I want is answers, none of your smart
     mouth.

Vince pulls Ronnie from the floor by the scruff of
his neck. Ronnie looks shocked.

                    VINCE (CONT'D)
                 (Close to Ronnie's face)
     You took my life from me Ron.

Vince punches Ronnie twice in the face, and then
throws him against the wall. Ronnie falls to the
floor this time his nose and lip are bleeding.

Ronnie is clearly annoyed at himself because he cannot control the situation.

> RONNIE
> *(To himself)*
Fuck.

> VINCE
> *(Interrogating)*
That night, I want to know what happened. Everything…

Vince pulls Ronnie's head back by his hair and moves in nose to nose.

> VINCE (CONT'D)
…And I want the truth. None of your fucking lies. The truth.

Vince violently pushes Ronnie's head away. It cracks against the wall.

> RONNIE
> *(Close to tears)*
What are you gonna do to me Vince?

> VINCE
> *(Aggressively)*
What would you do Ron?

Vince stands over Ronnie waiting.

> RONNIE
Alright, alright. Let me sort myself out.

Ronnie leans against the wall with one shoulder, holding the other arm in discomfort.

> RONNIE (CONT'D)
Charlie wanted you out the way. Do you know that?

> VINCE
> *(Confused)*
Charlie, why?

                    RONNIE
          Why do you think, you were with his
          daughter. He had control over the whole
          estate apart from you. You and your family.

Vince relaxes and looks out of the window at the
small estate they grew up on.

                    VINCE
          I lost everything I ever had over that shit
          hole!

                    RONNIE
          Charlie started up with some faces from the
          city. He cornered the drugs market here
          just as everyone got into it.

Ronnie shifts around a bit more to get comfortable
turning his back completely to Vince.

                    RONNIE (CONT'D)
          He knew how you felt about drugs Vince, we
          all did. You weren't gonna have none of it
          and he knew it.

Out of Vince's eye-line, Ronnie slips his mobile
from his pocket and flips it open.

                    RONNIE (CONT'D)
          You had to go Vince, simple as that.

Ronnie starts to dial, Vince sees him.

Vince moves to Ronnie and kicks the phone from his
grasp. Vince then stamps on Ronnie's hand, then
violently stamps a second time, this time breaking
Ronnie fingers.

Ronnie screams in agony. Vince grabs him by the
scruff of the neck again.

                    VINCE
          Play times over Ron. You're gonna talk, and
          your gonna do it now. My patience are
          running out fast.

Vince lets go and Ronnie fall to the floor holding
his broken hand.

                    VINCE (CONT'D)
This is it for you Ron, you do know that
don't ya. I can't let you get away with
that. I've spoken to Charlie, Lenny and
Lucy.

Vince looks on as Ronnie is in obvious pain.

                    VINCE (CONT'D)
I know why they done what they did. Now I
wanna know your reasons.

Ronnie shifts again to a more comfortable position
against the wall.

                    RONNIE
Alright.

Ronnie composes himself ready to talk.

                    RONNIE (CONT'D)
I fell in love with Lucy. I couldn't help
it, it just happened. When I started
working for Charlie, he had me drop
packages off to people. Yeah yeah, stupid I
know.

Vince listens.

                    RONNIE (CONT'D)
It was a way in Vince. I spent more and
more time around Charlie. I got a taste for
it. Plus, I got to see Lucy more. Sad I
know but all I saw was people give you
respect and I wanted some of that. All I
was, well, all I was, was that little mug
that tagged along with you. Nah not for me,
I wanted more.

Vince sits on some debris taking in what is being
said.

                    RONNIE (CONT'D)
I felt important. I was someone. I was me,
and not just Vince Nelson's little muggy
mate. The less time you and I spent
together made it easier. I knew what was
happening, I knew that if I was finally

gonna do something you had to be out the way.

                    VINCE
Why out the way? All you had to do was distance yourself.

                    RONNIE
And what? You'd of let me knock gear out on the estate? Do me a favor.

Vince knows it is the truth.

                    RONNIE (CONT'D)
Nah. Charlie had a plan. I felt guilty at first, but the promise of all that power was way too much. Plus, well you know, I was doing a bit myself. It was the in thing.

                    VINCE
Was it? I never touched the stuff.

                    RONNIE
That's why it wouldn't have worked.

Vince takes it in for a moment.

                    VINCE
What happened with Lucy?

                    RONNIE
When she told me she was pregnant, I knew right then I could have her. She couldn't tell Charlie it was yours, no way. I just wanted to be with her and at that point, she had no other choice. It was good at first, but I could tell all she wanted was you. I got jealous time after time. We drifted apart. The past ten years have been a charade. Honestly, the whole thing was a charade.

                    VINCE
Did you threaten Lenny?

> RONNIE
> *(In)*
> No. Charlie did. After you got nicked
> Charlie had to talk to Lenny, we weren't
> sure what he would say…

4   **INT. F/B THE MOON BACKROOM – NIGHT.**   4

The chairs are on the tables. Lenny sits on a stool
at the bar with Charlie and Ronnie standing in front
of him.

> CHARLIE
> *(With cigar)*
> See, you made the call Lenny. You made that
> call, what do you think Vince would say
> about that? If he found out that you set
> him up.

> LENNY
> *(Innocent)*
> I never set him up, tell him Ron.

> RONNIE
> You made the call Len, you did.

Lenny shakes his head scared and concerned.

> CHARLIE
> The old bill would nick ya. Vince would
> come after ya. Besides, who would look
> after your dear old Mum?

Lenny's eyes well up.

> CHARLIE (CONT'D)
> She's in a wheelchair ain't she?

> LENNY
> *(Nods)*
> Yeah.

> CHARLIE
> With no one to look out for her, she could
> have a nasty accident or something.

Lenny looks on petrified.

                    CHARLIE (CONT'D)
We don't want that to happen now, do we
Len?

                    LENNY
Please don't hurt my mum Mr Madigan.

                    CHARLIE
Me? I won't hurt her, why would I? In fact,
I have a job for you Lenny.

Charlie walks around the bar over Lenny's shoulder.

                    CHARLIE (CONT'D)
You can work here, for me.

Out on an upset Lenny.

5   **INT/EXT. BRICKYARD CONT'D – DAY.**   5

                    RONNIE (CONT'D)
…that was it. Lenny was in Charlie's pocket
like everyone else.

                    VINCE
                    (Disgusted)
How was I set up then?

                    RONNIE
I got Lenny pissed up and made him make
that call to you. Charlie and Patterson
done the rest.

                    VINCE
Patterson? I knew that snake was involved.

                    RONNIE
Charlie dealt Patterson in on the drugs,
and Patterson turned a blind eye. Another
one in his pocket. That's how it worked,
that's how it always worked.

Ronnie shifts uncomfortably.

                    RONNIE (CONT'D)
Charlie sent someone to the warehouse to do
the security guard. You know to make it
look like a robbery. Patterson supplied the

shotgun then acted on an anonymous tip off
when he got the call. It was literally as
easy as that.

Vince is angry.

                    RONNIE (CONT'D)
With Patterson in on it, you had no chance.

Vince grabs Ronnie.

                    VINCE
You were meant to be my mate. I looked out
for you.

Vince pushes Ronnie against the wall.

                    VINCE (CONT'D)
You could have done something to stop it
all.

                    RONNIE
                    (Smug)
Why should I of, I fucking despised you for
what you had.

                    VINCE
What I had? I had nothing.

Vince throws Ronnie to the floor and punches him.
Ronnie groans in pain and spits out some blood.

                    RONNIE
I think I should see someone about my hand
Vince, look at it.

Ronnie holds his broken fingers up almost deranged.

                    RONNIE (CONT'D)
I've seen that look in your eyes before.
Don't take it out on me, take it out on
Charlie, he's the one that concocted it
all.

                    VINCE
              (Picking Ronnie back up)
     I make you worse than him. I expect a prick
     like him to do something like that, but you
     were my mate.

Vince stamps on Ronnie's fingers again. Ronnie
squeals.

                    RONNIE
              (Protecting himself)
     What you gonna do now Vince, kill me?

Vince takes hold of Ronnie by the scruff of the neck
again.

                    RONNIE (CONT'D)
                (Panicking)
     Wait, wait, wait. There's more…

                    VINCE
                  (In)
     You're pathetic.

                    RONNIE
                (Quick)
     It's about your Dad.

Vince stops.

                    VINCE
     What?

                    RONNIE
     If I'm going down, then Charlie's coming
     with me.

Vince spins Ronnie around and throws him against the
debris.

                    VINCE
     What's my Dad got to do with all this?

Ronnie laughs as hysteria sets in.

                    VINCE (CONT'D)
     What are you fucking laughing at?

                    RONNIE
     Your gonna kill me. Your actually gonna
     kill me.

                    VINCE
     Yeah. I am.

Vince lets go, then stands over a helpless Ronnie.

                    VINCE (CONT'D)
     I wanna know about my Dad.

                    RONNIE
     The night your Dad died. It weren't as
     straight forward as it seemed.

Ronnie is ready to tell all.

                    RONNIE (CONT'D)
     Me, Charlie and Patterson were in the back
     room. Your Dad overheard Charlie talking
     about what we'd done to you…

6   **INT. F/B THE MOON PUB – NIGHT.**   6

VINCE'S DAD emerges from the toilet ready to make
his way back to the bar. He overhears voices in the
back room, and then moves to see.

Through the open door DAD NELSON'S POV.

                    CHARLIE
                  (With cigar)
     Casualty of war.

WE GO INTO A TWO SHOTS AND CLOSE UP'S.

They laugh. Ronnie pours drinks and offers them to
Charlie and Patterson.

                    PATTERSON
     Vince has no chance with his appeal. I've
     sorted that. We are home and dry.

                    CHARLIE
     This whole area's sewn up now. Ronnie give
     Mr Patterson his wages.

Ronnie drops an ENVELOPE on the table in front of Patterson. As Patterson moves to take it, he sees DAD NELSON now standing in the doorway.

Dad Nelson goes for Charlie.

                    DAD NELSON
                 (Fist clenched)
      You piece of shit.

Ronnie and Patterson intervene holding Dad Nelson.

Charlie casually walks toward the men as Dad Nelson struggles to free himself.

                    CHARLIE
      Oh dear, now we do have a problem.

                    DAD NELSON
                 (Gritted teeth)
      You're a dead man Charlie.

                    CHARLIE
                 (Smirking)
      Oh I don't think so do you? You'd have to
      go some to put one on me mate.

Dad Nelson turns to Ronnie.

                    DAD NELSON
      How have you got mixed up with this
      arsehole? How could you do it Ronnie?

                    CHARLIE
      These nice men are gonna show you to the
      door now. Make sure it's the last time you
      grace it, 'cause I'd hate for you to lose
      another one of your boy's.

CHARLIE SMILES PATRONISINGLY, KNOWING HE IS IN CONTROL OF EVERYTHING.

                    CHARLIE (CONT'D)
                 (Leaning in)
      You know what I mean?

Charlie opens the door for Ronnie and Patterson to escort Dad Nelson out.

They throw him to the floor at the top of the stairs that leads to the main bar. Lenny is at the foot of the stairs looking sheepish.

Dad Nelson pick's himself up knowing he is in a no win situation, and slowly heads down the stairs.

> DAD NELSON
> *(To Lenny)*
> Are you…

Before he can finish Charlie forces him down with his foot.

> CHARLIE
> And stay out!

Dad Nelson tumbles down the stairs and falls at a shocked Lenny's feet, then clutches his chest in pain.

Lenny bends to aid him as Ronnie runs down the stairs.

> LENNY
> *(Panicking, calling out)*
> Oh my God. Someone help him. Please, somebody call an ambulance.

Ronnie turns to the barmaid as she comes over to see what the commotion is.

> RONNIE
> *(To barmaid)*
> Call an ambulance.

She runs to the bar, Dad Nelson lays in Lenny's arms motionless. Lenny cries helplessly at the situation.

Ronnie looks up at Patterson and Charlie who stand at the top of the stairs.

Charlie smiles then exits, Patterson follows.

                    RONNIE (V.O.)
        …Charlie told everyone that he had the
        heart attack before he fell. Patterson
        backed him up. Nobody doubted them. That
        was it.

7   **INT/EXT. BRICKYARD CONT'D – DAY.**   7

CU Vince with tears rolling down his face. His face
turns to anger as he goes for Ronnie.

Vince starts to punch Ronnie in the face franticly.
Ronnie tries to protect himself by covering up.

                    VINCE
        My Dad. You killed my Dad. You wanker's.
        You dirty wanker's.

Vince continues to punch Ronnie franticly. Vince is
now like a wild animal.

Ronnie is thrown to the floor motionless. He is now
covered in blood, Vince sets about him again. Punch
after punch after punch, sprays of blood everywhere.

Vince stops, collapses onto Ronnie's dead body and
sobs.

Vince is in uncontrollable emotional pain.

WIDE SHOT.

Vince regains focus, lifts a lifeless Ronnie from
the floor and pushes him from the window.

Vince POV - Ronnie is now two stories down among the
rubble. Vince then sits with head in hands coming to
terms with what he has just done.

Vince gathers himself and sees the phone.

8   **INT. POLICE STATION – DAY.**   8

Patterson sits in the interview room as Delgado
appears with a folder containing photographic
evidence.

                        DELGADO
     We found Marcus Mitchell late last night.
     You know anything about this?

Delgado tosses the photos in front of Patterson.

Patterson glances at the photo of Marcus's dead
body, and then pushes them away.

                        PATTERSON
                        (Tired)
     No comment.

Delgado places crime scene photographs of Lenny's
dead body in front of Patterson.

                        DELGADO
     What about Lenny Hodge?

Patterson pushes them away without looking.

                        PATTERSON
     No comment. No comment. No comment. I've
     got nothing to say about anything.

Patterson sits with his head in his hands.

                        DELGADO
                        (Coolly)
     It doesn't matter really. We have all the
     evidence we need recorded.

                        PATTERSON
     You've got nothing.

                        DELGADO
                        (Smiling)
     Your friend Ronnie, talk about paranoid.

Delgado sits.

                    DELGADO (CONT'D)
     Did you see his CCTV set up? Quiet
     impressive really. Everywhere in that
     boozer has cameras. He could even monitor
     the toilet, and who to sell the coke to.
     Unbelievable.

                         PATTERSON
                     (Looking up)
     So, what's that got to do with me?

                         DELGADO
     You're little sessions in the back room.
     You, Charlie and Ronnie. Very cosy.

Patterson looks confused.

                    DELGADO (CONT'D)
                     (Explaining)
     Ronnie saw how callous you and Charlie
     were, so he started taping everything. You
     know, so he would have something to bargain
     with in case it all came on top for him.

Patterson puts his head back in his hands deflated.
Delgado leans in.

                    DELGADO (CONT'D)
                       (Cocky)
     See we've got you banged to rights. We've
     got you all banged to rights.

Out on Patterson defeated.

9   **INT. PUBLIC TOILETS – DAY.**   9

Vince is bare-chested washing the blood from his
hair, face and hands. The door opens and Freddie
appears with a holdall.

                         FREDDIE
                     (Walking in)
     I got here as quick as I could.

He sees the state of Vince.

                    FREDDIE (CONT'D)
     Fuck me, what's happened?

Vince opens the HOLDALL and hurriedly pulls out a towel to wipes his hands.

> VINCE
>
> I've fucked up Freddie. I've made a big mistake.

Vince fishes through the clothes in the bag.

> VINCE (CONT'D)
>
> Did you bring…

Freddie holds up an ENVELOPE.

Vince takes it flicks through the CASH and opens his PASSPORT.

> FREDDIE
> *(Starting to panic)*
> What have you done Vince? What's going on?

Vince starts getting changed. He cannot waste any time.

> VINCE
>
> It's Ronnie. He's dead.

> FREDDIE
> *(Confused)*
> Ronnie dead? How?

Vince looks at him, Freddie realises.

> FREDDIE (CONT'D)
> *(Scared)*
> You killed him. You killed Ronnie!

> VINCE
> *(Looking over to the door)*
> Keep your voice down.

Vince puts the cash and passport in his pocket then zips the HOLDALL up and puts it on his shoulder.

> VINCE (CONT'D)
>
> I've got to go somewhere quickly before I leave.

                         FREDDIE
          You're going away now?

                          VINCE
          I've got to.

Freddie pulls his own PASSPORT from his pocket.

                          VINCE
          What's that?

                         FREDDIE
          I'm coming with you!

                          VINCE
                    (Shocked)
          What?

                         FREDDIE
          I've got money. I won't get in your way.

                          VINCE
          No way Freddie.

Vince goes to the door. Freddie follows.

                         FREDDIE
          I'm coming, you can't stop me.

Vince throws Freddie against the wall knowing that
he cannot drag his little brother down with him.

                          VINCE
          Don't you understand I've got to go, I
          can't go back to prison. I just can't go
          back.

                         FREDDIE
                    (With a tear in his eye)
          I want to come with you Vince, there's
          nothing here for me.

Vince knows that he and Freddie share something
special but he cannot involve Freddie.

                          VINCE
          Freddie I can never come back here, do you
          understand that?

                    FREDDIE
        I just want to be with you. I'll do
        whatever you want me to do.

Vince needs to leave and knows the only way he can
get Freddie to stay is to play on his emotions.
Vince grabs Freddie by the throat.

                    VINCE
        Why would I want you with me, slowing me
        down? Leave me alone for fuck's sake.

Vince lets him go and heads for the door.

                    FREDDIE
                    (Crying)
        You don't mean that, we're brothers.

                    VINCE
        You don't even know me. You're not my
        brother, you mean nothing to me.

Vince looks on for a moment as Freddie stands there
broken hearted.

Freddie watches Vince leave.

CU of Vince standing outside the door as tears run
down his face, he hears Freddie sob inside then
moves out of frame.

10   **EXT. CHARLIE'S DRIVEWAY - DAY.**   10

        HIGH WIDE SHOT as Charlie is arrested by SCO19
        (Officers from Specialist Firearms Command unit)

        We go into a CU to see an expressionless Charlie.

        He is led to a car and then taken away.

11   **EXT. BRICKYARD - DAY.**   11

        The area around the derelict building has now been
        cordoned off with POLICE TAPE. There is a FORENSICS
        VEHICLE, an AMBULANCE and TWO POLICE VEHICLES. TWO
        POLICE OFFICERS are talking to THREE LADS about
        twelve years old as they point over to the crime
        scene.

12   INT. POLICE STATION – DAY.   12

Charlie sits casually in an interview room as
Delgado enters.

>   DELGADO
>
> Hello Charlie.

>   CHARLIE
>
> Am I supposed to know you?

>   DELGADO
>
> My name is DS Delgado, I'm here to ask you
> a few questions.

>   CHARLIE
>   *(Sitting back)*
>
> Is that right?

>   DELGADO
>
> Yeah. That's right.

The mood is broken as a PC enters.

>   PC
>   *(Handing over a piece of paper)*
>
> We've just found another one Guv.

The PC exits as Delgado looks at the paper.

>   DELGADO
>   *(Looking up at Charlie)*
>
> Well well, another one. Ronnie Keppel has
> just been found dead.

Charlie looks surprised for a moment then starts to
laugh.

>   DELGADO (CONT'D)
>
> What you laughing at? Did you just hear
> what I said? Your son in-law has been found
> dead, and all you do is laugh.

Delgado is disgusted.

>   CHARLIE
>
> Yeah yeah, I heard ya. Well I never thought
> he'd do it.

                    DELGADO
Who Charlie?

                    CHARLIE
                  (*Casually*)
Vince Nelson.

                    DELGADO
                 (*Leaning in*)
What did he do Charlie?

                    CHARLIE
                  (*Smiling*)
Ronnie. He murdered Ronnie.
Delgado looks over to an OFFICER in the
corner and nods indicating for him to act
on the information just given. The officer
exits swiftly.

                    DELGADO
                 (*Standing*)
This is not over Charlie.

Charlie smiles as Delgado exits.

13   **INT. NELSON'S HOUSE – DAY.**   13

Jack runs through the door where George, Frank and
Billy are waiting.

                    JACK
                 (*Panicking*)
What's going on?

                    GEORGE
I don't know. Freddie rang me and said he
wanted us all to be here. He sounded shook.

                    JACK
Where's Vince?

                    GEORGE
I don't know he left earlier.

                    JACK
What else did Freddie say?

                    GEORGE
     He was brief. I think he was running. He
     seemed out of breath.

The door bursts opens and an out of breath Freddie
runs in.

                    BILLY
                (Going to Freddie)
     Take a breath Freddie. What's going on?

Frank moves a chair around for Freddie to sit on.

                    FREDDIE
     It's Vince.

George puts his head in his hands knowing something
bad has happened.

                    FRANK
     Is he alright?

The brothers look concerned.

                    FREDDIE
                (Frantic)
     He's done something bad.

                    BILLY
                (Calming)
     Ok Fred.

Billy puts a reassuring hand on Freddie's shoulder
and looks at George.

                    BILLY (CONT'D)
     Take your time mate.

                    FREDDIE
                (Standing)
     That's just the thing we ain't got any
     time. Vince has gone.

                    JACK
                (In)
     What do you mean gone? Gone where?

                    FREDDIE
                   (Pacing)
     He took his passport and went.

                    GEORGE
                   (Standing)
     He couldn't of done, I've been here all day
     and he ain't…

The penny drops.

                    GEORGE (CONT'D)
                   (Disappointed)
     Oh no, Freddie.

                    FREDDIE
                   (Confused)
     He told me not to say anything. I thought
     I'd done the right thing.

Freddie sits and puts his head in his hands.

                    FREDDIE (CONT'D)
     I've fucked it all up.

                    GEORGE
                   (Moving to him)
     What did he do Freddie?

Freddie takes a moment then faces his brothers.

                    FREDDIE
                   (Sad)
     He killed Ronnie.

The boys are stunned.

14   INT. KEPPEL'S HOUSE – DAY.   14

TWO POLICE OFFICER'S stand in the dining room, Lucy
is sitting at the table stunned at what she has just
heard. Sammy is in disbelief.

                    OFFICER 1
                   (Solemn)
     That's all we know at this time Mrs Keppel.
     I'm sorry.

Sammy rocks against the wall as the officers look on
helplessly at their distress.

                    OFFICER 2
                    (Sombre)
        If there is anything you need.

Lucy moves to comfort Sammy.

                    SAMMY
                    (Hard)
        Get your fucking hands off me you slag.

Sammy pushes Lucy to the floor. The officers
restrain Sammy.

                 SAMMY (CONT'D)
           (Struggling to free himself)
        Get your fucking hands off me. Let go of
        me.

                    OFFICER 1
        Calm down Mr Keppel, please calm down.

Lucy looks on, Sammy look at Lucy.

                    OFFICER 2
        If we let you go, you have to promise not
        to do anything silly.

Referring to attacking his mother.

                    SAMMY
                 (Staring at her)
        I don't want anything to do with her, let
        me get out of here.

They cautiously let him go. He leaves the room
smashing things from the table. The officers and
Lucy watch him leave.

                    LUCY
            (Nervous and embarrassed)
        You said Vince Nelson is a named suspect.
        Named by who?

The officers look at one another.

                    OFFICER 1
                   (Awkward)
     Mrs Keppel, your father is being questioned
     as we speak. He Named Mr Nelson.

                    OFFICER 2
     We are still trying to pick Mr Nelson up
     for questioning. As yet we've had no luck
     locating him.

They look at a deflated Lucy.

                     LUCY
                  (Anguished)
     I know where he'll be.

The officers look at one another.

                  LUCY (CONT'D)
     Take me with you and let me talk to him.

                    OFFICER 1
     Mrs Keppel normally…

                     LUCY
                  (Cutting in)
     Look, I can defuse the situation. Let me
     talk to him.

The officers share another look. They have nothing
to lose.

                    OFFICER 2
     Ok. Where?

                     LUCY
             (Putting her coat on)
     He'll be at St Augustine's church by the
     canal.

Officer 1 radios through the information as they
exit.

We pan across to see Sammy emerge from behind the
door.

15   INT. NELSON'S HOUSE CONT'D - DAY.   15

The brothers are in the same position we last saw
them in.

                         FRANK
          He'll be long gone by now.

                         BILLY
          What else did he say?

                         FREDDIE
          Nothing, that was it.

                         JACK
                    (To George)
          What do we do?

                         FRANK
                    (To Freddie)
          Did he give you any clues to where he might
          have gone?

                         FREDDIE
          Nah. He just said he has to go away and
          that he can't come back. That was it.

The boys are lost.

                         FREDDIE (CONT'D)
          He said he had one more place to go before
          he went though.

The boys look at one another.

                         GEORGE
                    (Breaking the silence, sure)
          I know where he is.

The boys look at one another and make to leave in a
hurry.

16   INT/EXT. POLICE CAR - DAY.   16

MOS.

The police drive full speed. The officers are on the
radio and the BLUES ARE ON.

Lucy gazes out of the window helplessly.

17 **EXT. NELSON'S HOUSE – DAY.** 17

MOS.

The Nelson's get into the rover and speed off.

As they EXIT FRAME LEFT, TWO SQUAD CARS AND A POLICE VAN ENTER FRAME RIGHT and race around the corner screeching to a stop outside the Nelson's house.

18 **EXT. GRAVEYARD – DAY.** 18

Tranquilly Vince stands over the family grave unaware of the mayhem about to unfold.

We TRACK slowly around Vince.

> VINCE (V.O.)
> My life has never really been easy. In fact I've been running and hiding for as long as I can remember. I never wanted to come back. I suppose I never wanted to find out the truth. I must have owed it to myself or something, who knows. I love you Mum, and not a day goes by that I don't think about you and all you done for us. Dad, I'm so sorry I missed you. It wasn't my fault, but I beat myself up every day thinking that I wish I'd been there for you. I let you down, and I can never make it right. Danny, I feel so sad that I never really had a chance to know you. You're at rest now with people that love you. I wish I could stay here with you all forever…

The sound of a car screeching around the corner halts Vince's words. He turns to look.

It's his brothers. They get out of the car.

> GEORGE
> (Calling out)
> Vince, wait.

Vince is torn between running away or to his brothers.

                         VINCE
          Don't try and stop me. I've got to go.

The brothers move towards Vince.

                         GEORGE
          We're not here to stop you.

They move closer, we hear SIRENS in the distance.

                         VINCE
                      (Panicking)
          I'm running out of time.

                         GEORGE
          We'll hold them up.

The SIRENS are now really close.

                         GEORGE (CONT'D)
          Take care Vince.

SLOW MOTION.

They all share a moment.

The boys' eyes quickly look to Vince's right.

                         FRANK
                      (Panic-stricken)
          No!

The brothers all look shocked.

Before Vince can turn, he sees his brothers sprayed
with blood. He looks confused for a moment then
looks down. His own body is GUSHING BLOOD. His face
turns to horror as he staggers then collapses to his
knees.

His brothers take cover as we hear a SECOND GUNSHOT,
they flinch again as we hear the THIRD, all three
hitting Vince.

In the background, we can see the POLICE ARRIVING IN
DROVES.
SCO19 are screaming for everyone to stay on the
ground.

We see Freddie get up, run to Vince and cradle him.
Vince is covered in blood and struggling to breath.

SCO19 move past them and shout for someone to
disarm.

We see Lucy get out of a police car and run toward
the scene hysterically.
She is stopped, and then restrained for her own
safety.

We move around the group to see SCO19 SURROUNDING
SAMMY KEPPEL as he drops his FIREARM.

He is thrown to the floor and HANDCUFFED.

The brother's go to Vince as Freddie cradles him.

REAL TIME - the scene is chaotic as the police try
to restore order.

                    FREDDIE
                   (Crying)
      Please Vince, please. No, no.

Vince is motionless. George pulls Freddie away as
PARAMEDICS move in. it is too late.

George comforts Freddie. He sobs uncontrollably. The
brothers are distraught.

THE CAMERA MOVES WIDER AND WIDER TO REVEAL THE
ENTIRE SCENE AS DON MCLEAN'S 'VINCENT' SOFTLY PLAYS.

REFLECTION: CLOSING MONOLOGUE

So, that was my brother's story. Vince Nelson, he truly was a man amongst men and one who definitely wore his heart on his sleeve. Troubled for sure, but then again, ain't we all? It's safe to say that Vince would never have let you down, ever. He always did protest his innocence, for years he insisted he was never meant to be there the night he was arrested. I guess he was telling the truth. He really didn't deserve what he got, in fact he didn't deserve any of it. Not a day goes by that I don't think about what could have been for all of us, what he himself could have been if things were different. This family has been torn apart, first mum, then dad, and then Danny and Vince in quick succession. A few years after that day Billy was found dead in his flat. He drank himself to death. He had plenty of warning signs, but like most, he chose to ignore them. Frank, well what can I say about Frank? He's still plodding along, a bit older and a bit wiser. Moved down to Eastbourne, bigger house, more money, same old same old. Even Jack ended up settling down, three kids and four stone married, you know the story.

Last I heard about Patterson, he ended up extending his stay at Her Majesty's pleasure, no less than he deserved really, we've not seen him around this estate since then, good job too. Lucy moved away shortly after that day, up north I heard, Preston or somewhere like that. Sammy joined her once he came out by all accounts, not that anyone cares. Charlie on the other hand was never heard of again. Rumour has it he turned Queens, grassed up some big names. Seems about right for a snake like that really.

The one shining light throughout all of it was Freddie, what a fantastic man he has turned out to be. He moved out to Thailand with Vince's old business partner and ran the bar for a few years, before opening his own place in Australia. He now has a chain of restaurants and bars along the Gold Coast. Put it this way, I wouldn't mind being a pound-note behind him. As for me, I still live here. Crazy I know after all that's happened. But if I'm honest, I haven't really got anywhere else to be. Besides, who else was going to finish the story?

CREDITS ROLL.

FADE TO BLACK.

About the author

Daniel R. Lee

Daniel R. Lee (Danny) was born into a hardworking, middle-class family in the winter of 1970. He grew up on a locally distinguished council estate near Croydon in South London called New Addington. His early teenage years were spent at the Monks Hill High Comprehensive School. It was an education that was not only academic, but also personable and social.

Danny followed his father, Dickie Lee, into the British film industry where he spent the first fifteen years of his working life. He learnt his trade at Cine Europe Ltd, a prestigious 16mm camera rental house in White City London. Here he gained the fundamental knowledge that enabled him to go freelance as a Clapper Loader on TV and film productions. Danny then worked on several productions around the world as a Clapper Loader, Focus Puller and then briefly as a Camera Operator. It was here he met his wife, who was an actress on one of the productions he was working on. Knowing the demands and strain the industry can put on relationships, he decided to leave filmmaking behind and support his wife's acting career, whilst pursuing other lines of work, predominantly towards sport.

An HGV licence helped to bolster his earnings whilst studying for a range of qualifications specific to the football industry. Danny has since gained experience working for a number of professional and semi-professional football clubs, and as a senior county match official. After a prestigious offer to work abroad at a professional football club, his dream was brought down to earth due to his lack of academic qualifications. This setback was needless to say, taken as a challenge and his academic journey was underway. Danny accessed university through a Foundation Degree in Sports Coaching at the University of Roehampton, which developed in to a Batchelor of Arts Sports Coaching degree at the same institution. (The photographs in this book were taken as part of a social regeneration research project in that degree programme). Danny's hard work and resilience resulted in him being asked to become a guest lecturer on the BA Sports Coaching programme at Roehampton. During this time, Danny created a sports coaching company, largely around football, offering an exit route through education for young adolescent males. This was designed to help raise education statistics and lower crime in the local area.

As a lifelong learner, Danny then decided to undertake a Master's degree at the University of Central Lancashire. This is where he met Dr Clive Palmer, who was his supervisor for his final dissertation. This became Danny's first academic publication, *Hatch, Match and Dispatch: a creative but nonfictional journey through research methods (Lee and Palmer, 2018, in the Journal of Qualitative Research in Sports Studies).* Knowing that Danny had an inquiring mind, Clive helped Danny to take his learning to the next level of PhD where Clive is currently his Director of Studies. For his current research and having gained an insight to Danny's extensive past, a PhD project was envisaged that embraced Danny's talents as a creative and strategic thinker, along with his background as a filmmaker. Danny's PhD is an investigation of performance cultures and group dynamics in sport, using narrative and film documentaries as creative ways to collect data and communicate his discoveries. The Nelson Boys, whilst entirely fictional, is an exercise in to scripted data analysis which will be used in his PhD; with multiple voices and perspectives brought together to focus on a theme or social setting. In 2018-19 Danny was a Senior Lecturer in Sport and Physical Education for University of Central Lancashire, based in Changsha, Hunan Province, China, after which he returned to the UK to commence with his research and sports-business interests.

About the Editor

Clive Palmer

Clive Palmer is a Senior Lecturer in Sport and Physical Education at the University of Central Lancashire. He draws upon his varied background in sport, engineering, the arts and philosophy to experiment with teaching ideas and creatively engage learners in their studies. Towards promoting academic confidence, he publishes student-centred writing which is where Clive's partnership with Danny started and brought this book in to being. Underpinning Clive's interests for physicality in learning, Clive has competed at national level in three sports; gymnastics, athletics and canoeing. From being an Apprentice Engineer in the RAF, he became a school teacher and since 2000, he has been lecturer and curriculum designer-come-research supervisor in Higher Education. From these experiences, Clive believes in the transferability of skills and importantly, that a university degree is primarily for educating the person, not solely for knowledge acquisition… and that it should be a fun learning experience.

A strong advocate of Research Informed Teaching and recognising student-voice in the education process, Clive has pursued his ideas for learning through literacy and arts-based teaching. In 2007, he established the *Journal of Qualitative Research in Sports Studies* (ISSN 1754-2375) as an 'academic window' for social research in sport. Across 12 volumes to date, 126 articles from national and international scholars stand shoulder-to-shoulder to inform the curriculum or others' learning, wherever that may be globally. Clive is also Editor of the Sporting Image Series of eight books of creative writing. This ground-breaking work affords a view into an arts-based pedagogy, which 'goes public' to share good practice and inspire new learners.

Recognising the vocational-academic divide in HE for studying Outdoor Leadership, Sport and Physical Education, Clive has been influential for curriculum change across undergraduate and postgraduate study. A Senior Fellow of the Higher Education Academy in the UK, he is also Visiting Professor to Hunan Normal University in Changsha, China, to promote cross-cultural research between staff and students by learning through Physical Education. His catalogue of student-centred work is now accessed by 100s of thousands of students and teachers around the world, and attracts contributions from as far afield as Australia, China, South Africa, Germany, Greece, America, Canada, and many British universities.

Some previous titles include:

Journal of Qualitative Research in Sports Studies (2007-date)

Arts-Based Education in Outdoor Learning:
The Outdoor Image (2019)

The Sports Monograph: Critical Perspectives on Socio-cultural
Sport, Coaching and Physical Education (2014)

The Sporting Image: Unsung Heroes of the
Olympics 1896-2012 (2013)

The Role of Sports in the Formation of Personal Identities:
Studies in Community Loyalties (2012)

The Sporting Image: The Abstraction of Form in Sport.
A Collection of Art with Supporting Narratives (2011)

The Sporting Image: What If? An Anthology of Creative Writing
Based Upon Real-life Events in Sport (2010)

The Sporting Image: Sports Poetry and
Creative Writing (2009)

The Turn to Aesthetics: An Interdisciplinary Exchange of Ideas
in Applied and Philosophical Aesthetics (2008)

Further Information

A range of further information is available at the Nelson Boys website and at other links below, which are relevant to the development of the Nelson Boys as a screenplay, but also to new and related areas that have evolved from the experience of producing this book. These include writing for an audience in scripted form, to becoming a PhD researcher in socio-cultural sport.

The Nelson Boys

- http://thenelsonboys.co.uk

- Nelson Boys comments page, character profiles and pictures.

- Would you like to see The Nelson Boys on TV?

- Author and Editor additional information / links

- Notification of new scripts by Daniel R. Lee

- Socio-cultural research links: storytelling in qualitative research, narrative, ethnography, photo-novella, reflexive writing…

Danny Lee

- Sports Education and Training Ltd: http://www.sportset.org.uk

- Next Generation Pro Football Academy: http://www.ngpfa.com

- Lee, D. and Palmer, C. (2018) Hatch, match and dispatch: a creative but nonfictional journey through research methods. *Journal of Qualitative Research in Sports Studies*, 12, 1, 101-166.

Clive Palmer (Full vitae and publications)

- Links to all journal papers (JQRSS) and all creative writing books by chapter at Academia.edu: https://uclan.academia.edu/ClivePalmer/

- Dane Valley Press – updates on publications

Would you like to see The Nelson Boys on TV?

We are starting a campaign of support for The Nelson Boys,
one that you could help promote.

Please visit the website
www.thenelsonboys.co.uk
to show your support.